MW00454276

Age of Discovery

A Captivating Guide to an Era of Exploration in European History, Including Discoveries Such as Christopher Columbus' Voyages to the Americas and Vasco da Gama's Sea Route to India

© Copyright 2019

All Rights Reserved. No part of this book may be reproduced in any form without permission in writing from the author. Reviewers may quote brief passages in reviews.

Disclaimer: No part of this publication may be reproduced or transmitted in any form or by any means, mechanical or electronic, including photocopying or recording, or by any information storage and retrieval system, or transmitted by email without permission in writing from the publisher.

While all attempts have been made to verify the information provided in this publication, neither the author nor the publisher assumes any responsibility for errors, omissions or contrary interpretations of the subject matter herein.

This book is for entertainment purposes only. The views expressed are those of the author alone, and should not be taken as expert instruction or commands. The reader is responsible for his or her own actions.

Adherence to all applicable laws and regulations, including international, federal, state and local laws governing professional licensing, business practices, advertising and all other aspects of doing business in the US, Canada, UK or any other jurisdiction is the sole responsibility of the purchaser or reader.

Neither the author nor the publisher assumes any responsibility or liability whatsoever on the behalf of the purchaser or reader of these materials. Any perceived slight of any individual or organization is purely unintentional.

Free Bonus from Captivating History
(Available for a Limited time)

Hi History Lovers!

Now you have a chance to join our exclusive history list so you can get your first history ebook for free as well as discounts and a potential to get more history books for free! Simply visit the link below to join.

Captivatinghistory.com/ebook

Also, make sure to follow us on Facebook, Twitter and Youtube by searching for Captivating History.

Table of Contents

Introduction

The Age of Discovery began in the early part of the 15th century and carried on through most of the 17th century. It is sometimes also referred to as the Age of Exploration. This was a time when the people of Europe began to travel, discover, and explore more of the world than ever before, mapping and naming the places they found. They bravely went out on the seas to learn about the world, often never sure if they would find anything at all, let alone ever return home.

The explorations made during this time would impact the shape of the world going forward in many ways. Colonization, trade, and education all changed due to the expansion of the known world, as well as international relationships. The Age of Discovery was an exciting time for everyone in Europe, from navigators and mapmakers to monarchs and merchants. Eager to forge new trade routes between their own kingdoms and exotic lands, kings and queens invested in maritime exploration, hoping to find valuable goods that could boost flatlining local economies.

The European economy shifted from land-based wealth to a market based largely on hordes of gold and silver. Even the poorest of people eventually benefited from trade with India, China, southern Asia, and the New World, where highly efficient crops such as potatoes and corn were exported. Whereas traditional cereal crops yielded about ten bushels of grain per acre, corn provided closer to twenty bushels—thus, agriculture was forever changed, boosting local populations in just a few short generations.[1]

Great navigators and explorers like Christopher Columbus, Prince Henry the Navigator, Walter Raleigh, and many, many more thrived during this period of history, not only making names for themselves but also bringing untold treasures home to their monarchs and families. It was an inevitable and climactic era that would leave no family, no country, and no landmass the same.

---

[1] Nelson, Lynn H. "The Impact of Discovery on Europe." Department of History, University of Kansas. 26 February 1998.

Chapter 1 – Prince Henry the Navigator

The Portuguese were the first Europeans to set sail on multi-year voyages, and Prince Henry is considered to be a pivotal figure in the Age of Discovery. Prince Henry (Infante Dom Henrique of Portugal, Duke of Viseu) was born on March 4th, 1394, and he would come to be known as Prince Henry the Navigator.[2]

The Portuguese were not the only ones on the seas at the time. The Spaniards and the Italians had also been in the Mediterranean for a long time, but the Portuguese were clearly the first to venture off on journeys that would leave the security of visible land or well-traveled routes behind them. Under Prince Henry, those heading out to sea were encouraged to go farther and find out what was in the unmapped world, especially if finding a new route to get to the West African trade was a result of the exploration.

Prince Henry encouraged his father, King John I, to capture Ceuta, a port in Morocco, as it was negatively affecting the Portuguese. There were pirates basing themselves there that were continually raiding the Portuguese coastline nearby and taking Portuguese people as slaves to

---

[2] Russell, P.E. *Prince Henry 'the Navigator': A Life.* 2001.

be sold for profit. After the successful taking of Ceuta, an emboldened Prince Henry put his efforts into exploring along the coast of Africa. He was keen on discovering where the West African gold trade was.

Portugal's seafaring ventures meant there needed to be some changes to the way they were currently accessing the water. The boats they were using were very heavy, which made them very slow as well. Overall, these boats were also quite fragile and hard to maneuver. They had one single square sail, and they weighed up to two hundred tons, which, one can imagine, did not handle the wind well. Henry wanted new ships that were lighter and better able to navigate the seas more quickly.

At this point, the Portuguese caravel was developed. This new vessel was actually based largely on the fishing boats already in use in Portugal. It was much more suited to the desired southern sea voyages. These new ships were easier to navigate, lighter, and had up to three masts with triangular sails rather than the old square ones. With the speed, better maneuverability, and the capacity to sail in more shallow coastal waters, Prince Henry and the Portuguese began their explorations. One of the first accomplishments of their journeys brought about the spice trade between Spain and Portugal.

It was during Prince Henry's time that the navigators of Portugal learned about the trade winds in the North Atlantic. With the knowledge of how the wind patterns affected travel on the different routes and how to use these patterns to their advantage, the navigators of the Age of Discovery advanced the world of ocean navigation in a big way. Sailing from Europe off into the North Atlantic or south to West Africa was done in a more predictable manner than was possible before understanding the recurring wind patterns. This advancement was something that all future oceanic voyagers would utilize henceforth.

In 1418, two explorers under King John I's commission were blown off course in a storm as they returned from a mission to explore along the African coast.[3] They found refuge at an island near Madeira, and they named it Porto Santo. After they reported it to King John, Prince Henry insisted it be claimed and colonized, most likely to claim it before the Kingdom of Castile did, as they'd recently laid claim to the Canary Islands.

Prince Henry's desire to explore the world, to map beyond the currently known lands, and to learn more about the coasts of Africa continually spurred him and Portuguese sailing efforts to find a route to China via the water, as well as to access trading partners directly and to find gold and valuables that would not only make Portugal richer but would also continue to fund more explorations.

In 1434, the Portuguese sailed beyond Cape Bojador on the northern coast of Western Sahara, with Gil Eanes in command of one of Henry's expeditions. Up to that point, Cape Bojador had basically been considered the end of the earth, and there were stories that there were only sea monsters to be found past it. In a time of superstition and the lack of knowledge to dispel the myths, the fear of sea monsters and the end of the earth was a valid reason to avoid sailing there.

The explorations of Prince Henry and his Portuguese discoverers found the Bay of Arguin in 1443, and by 1448, they'd built a fort there.[4] They crossed the Senegal River and went around the Cap-Vert (Cape Verde) Peninsula, discovered the Azores, and helped Portugal grow rich with the influx of gold and slaves. Henry accomplished one of his biggest goals, which was to find a route that bypassed the Muslim trade routes. Even though Prince Henry was dead by November 1460, his sponsored explorations had strongly built the foundations for future Portuguese discovery efforts, and they eventually did find a route to India via the Cape of Good Hope,

---

[3] Diffie, B., *Foundations of the Portuguese Empire.* 1977.
[4] Major, R., *The Life of Prince Henry of Portugal, Surnamed the Navigator; and its Results.* 1868.

which was discovered in the south of Africa under Bartolomeu Dias in 1488.

Chapter 2 – Bartolomeu Dias

The next great explorer of the Portuguese Age of Discovery era was Bartolomeu Dias (also known as Bartholomew Diaz). He was born in 1450 and would build on the seafaring explorations of Prince Henry the Navigator. Under King John II, Dias would take Portugal even further into the new world. Dias is usually thought to be one of the greatest Portuguese explorers from the 15th century.[5]

History has little information about Bartolomeu Dias prior to his entry into the world of sailing. It is thought that he worked in the royal warehouses of the king, and speculation indicates that he was descended somehow from Prince Henry the Navigator.[6] There is only one recorded instance of Dias participating in a sailing expedition prior to being put at the head of King John II's crew looking for a sea route to India in 1486. The Portuguese had learned of Prince Ogane, who they possibly confused with the Christian Prester John, but they hoped he would be an ally against the Muslims. John II sent Pêro da Covilhã and Afonso de Paiva off to find him in India or Abyssinia. Their travel was overland, while Dias was given the task of finding a similar route but via the water. He was to meet up with Covilhã and

---

5 Britannica
6 Britannica

Paiva once he got there. The search for a way to navigate around the southernmost tip of Africa via the water was still very much the biggest goal for the Portuguese.

Dias headed off from Lisbon in August of 1487, heading along the coast of South Africa.[7] Three ships made up Dias' sailing fleet for the expedition. He was aboard the *São Cristóvão*, João Infante headed the *São Pantaleão*, and Dias' brother Pêro was on the third ship, which was a supply ship carrying the food stores needed for the voyage.

Dias took six Africans along with them and traveled the route of Diogo Cão up to Cape Cross, Namibia. As he sailed along the African coast, Dias dropped the Africans off, and they ventured inland with gold and silver to show goodwill from the Portuguese to any of the indigenous tribes they found there. At the spot they left the last two Africans, in possibly what is now Angola, Bartolomeu Dias decided to leave his brother and the supply ship and placed nine of his men there to guard it while they continued with the expedition.

As the Portuguese ships sailed along the coast, they left markers mostly made of limestone. They called these markers *padrões*, and they served two purposes. Firstly, they could be used as guideposts for other Portuguese ships coming after them. Secondly, the markers showed that the Portuguese were claiming this route as their own, as well as the corresponding coast.

In January of 1488, after severe storms blew them from their course, Dias made some risky moves to deal with the southeasterly winds to avoid ending up on the rocky coast.[8] Fortuitously, land was spotted, and the men found that the bay they'd come into had the warm waters of the Indian Ocean. Unfortunately, the indigenous people in that spot were not welcoming and threw rocks at the

---

[7] Macleod, A. *Explorers: Tales of Endurance and Exploration*. DK Smithsonian. 2012.

[8] Swanson, J., *Bartolomeu Dias: First European Sailor to Reach the Indian Ocean*. 2017.

intruders, and Dias' men considered the risks of continuing, including their meager food stocks that were left. Dias wisely allowed a council of sailors to make the decision, and they agreed to let him travel three more days before turning back. They continued those three days, and on March 12th, 1488, they placed a limestone marker that would now show Portugal's most easterly explored area.[9] Also, on their return trip, they would mark the most southern point for the Portuguese to have traveled, which was Cape Needles and the Cape of Storms, thus named by Dias for its terrible weather and strong currents that had made their travel difficult and risky.

When Dias and his crew returned to the supply ship they'd left behind, they were shocked to find that the men guarding the ship had been repeatedly attacked by the indigenous people living there. There were only three of the nine men left alive, and one of those would still die on the way home.

Overall, this journey took Bartolomeu Dias a total of 16,000 miles and at least a year and three months to complete, although there has been speculation that it took longer. They were met with crowds celebrating their return, and Dias convened with King John II to report on his expedition. It appears that the king was not entirely pleased with Dias, however. Dias did not meet up with Covilhã and Paiva as was his original mission; in fact, while Covilhã reported in on his news from his travels to India and through Africa, and of what he found out about the spice trade and what he thought may help with the route via the sea, Paiva had died before meeting back up with Covilhã, so their mission was somewhat unsuccessful. The king renamed Dias' Cape of Storms as the Cape of Good Hope, and he did not send him out in charge of an expedition again.

Dias settled down for some time in West Africa at Guinea, as the Portuguese had established a gold trading settlement there. Later, when King John II had been succeeded by King Manuel I,

---

[9] Stein, S., *The Sea in World History; Exploration, Travel and Trade*. 2017.

Bartolomeu Dias would find himself called back to serve the Portuguese king in the business of sea exploration. He was tasked with supervising the building of the ships to be used in Vasco da Gama's expedition in 1497.[10] Dias sailed with da Gama part of the way, and he would also later sail with Pedro Álvares Cabral, who would go on to travel all the way to Brazil in 1500.[11]

Dias died in late May of 1500 when the ship he was on was lost in a storm ironically near what Dias himself had named the Cape of Storms in 1488.[12]

[10] Paine, L., *Ships of Discovery and Exploration.* 2000.
[11] Sadlier, D., *Brazil Imagined: 1500 to the Present.* 2010.
[12] Friedman, J. and Figg, K., *Trade, Travel, and Exploration in the Middle Ages.* 2013.

Chapter 3 – Vasco da Gama

Vasco da Gama was the next Portuguese explorer to take to the seas in the quest for new discoveries and advancements into the unmapped world. Da Gama was born sometime between 1460 and 1469 to a minor nobleman who was in command of the fortress of Sines, which was in the southwest of Portugal.[13]

In 1492, King John II sent da Gama to go against the French at the Portuguese city of Setúbal and the region of Algarve.[14] There, he seized French ships as retribution for French attacks that had been made during peacetime with Portugal. Da Gama completed this mission in good order, and the king was pleased.

Da Gama was not the most experienced or knowledgeable person to put at the head of such an important military engagement, but the da Gama family seemed to have the favor of the court and thus received many positions.

Da Gama was not only the first Portuguese but was, in fact, also the first European to actually reach India via the sea. Once this sea route to India was found, the Atlantic and Indian Oceans were finally linked

---

[13] Ames, G., *Vasco Da Gama: Renaissance Crusader*. 2005.
[14] Ibid.

as a travel route for trade. As in past explorations, this expedition also sought to disrupt the trade monopoly the Muslims held with the East.

Vasco da Gama's historic voyage set sail from Lisbon on July 8th, 1497.[15] He had in his fleet four ships. They were the São Gabriel, which he would command; the São Rafael, which was to be commanded by his brother Paulo da Gama; the São Miguel (also called Berrio), which was commanded by Nicolau Coelho; and a supply ship commanded by Gonçalo Nunes. The São Gabriel and São Rafael were medium-sized ships with three masts. The Berrio was a caravel, and the supply ship was a large, heavy vessel that weighed two hundred tons.

The expedition reached the Cape Verde Islands by July 26th, and da Gama decided to keep them there until August before venturing farther.[16] He took a longer route south, hoping to avoid unfavorable currents from the Gulf of Guinea before embracing the challenge of the Cape of Good Hope. More strong currents and winds delayed further advancement, and the fleet didn't round the Cape of Good Hope until November 22nd.[17]

Da Gama and his fleet reached the coast of Natal, South Africa, on Christmas Day of 1497 after the long stop-and-start voyage, and by January 11th, 1498, they had reached the Rio do Cobre (Copper River) near modern Mozambique, where they anchored for five days.[18] By January 25th, the fleet needed to stop. They had reached the River of Good Omens in Mozambique, and with the crew suffering dreadfully from scurvy and the ships needing repairs, they stayed in place for a month.

When da Gama and his ships finally sailed as far as the Island of Mozambique in early March, the people there took them to be Muslims. These people were themselves Muslims and shared their

---

[15] Ibid.
[16] World Exploration from Ancient Times, Encyclopedia Britannica, Inc.
[17] Ibid.
[18] Ibid.

information quite freely with da Gama. They explained their trade practices and told them about the Arab merchants with their ships filled with treasures. They also told him about the Christian Prester John the Portuguese had been seeking for some time. Da Gama was entrusted with two pilots from the sultan of Mozambique who would assist with further navigation.

By April 7th, the fleet arrived at Mombasa and took on another pilot who would guide them to Calicut on the coast of India. It took them 23 days to sail across the Indian Ocean and for India itself to finally come into sight. Da Gama put up a stone *padrão* (pillar) to ensure there was proof he'd finally succeeded in reaching the long-sought-after Indian coast.[19]

Da Gama did not receive the gracious reception he'd had in Mozambique, though. He'd assumed he would be met by Christians. But here, the people were Hindu. The Zamorin, the ruler of Calicut, was unimpressed by the goods the Portuguese brought for trade. While they were quite sufficient for the trade in West Africa, they were thought to be cheap and unsuitable for this new market. The Zamorin found da Gama rude, and the Muslim merchants were hostile toward the newly arrived Portuguese who were intent on taking up trade there.

Da Gama tried unsuccessfully to make a trade treaty after finally reaching India. By August, he and his fleet set sail to go home. Having no experience in sailing from this part of the continent, da Gama, unfortunately, set out during monsoon season. It took three months to sail across the Arabian Sea, and he lost much of his crew to scurvy. At Malindi, 120 kilometers north of Mombasa, da Gama had the São Rafael burned as he no longer had the crew to man all the ships. The remaining ships finally returned to Mozambique on February 1st, 1499, and the Cape of Good Hope on March 20th.

---

[19] "Padrao." *Encyclopedia Britannica.* Web.

Da Gama was ready finally to return to Portugal, but his ships preceded him as he stayed behind on Santiago Island with his dying brother Paulo, who had commanded the São Rafael. Paulo would not survive the completion of the expedition, dying in either June or July 1499.

Vasco da Gama accomplished what the Portuguese discovery expeditions had sought to do from the start. He'd successfully found the route to India that the Portuguese could now use for trade. Unfortunately, he'd not been able to negotiate a trade treaty with Calicut, and he'd lost more than half the men he'd taken on the voyage and returned with only two of the four ships he'd left with.

Da Gama's new route to India would subsequently be traveled yearly by the Portuguese for trade. Another consequence of da Gama's expedition was that the Portuguese would come to understand the value the eastern coast of Africa would have for them—an understanding that led to the colonization of Mozambique.

Chapter 4 – Albuquerque

Afonso de Albuquerque was another of the great Portuguese explorers during the Age of Discovery. He was born in 1453 near Lisbon, Portugal.[20] On Albuquerque's father's side, both his grandfather and his great-grandfather had served as secretaries to the king (King John I and King Edward, also known as Duarte). On his mother's side, Albuquerque's grandfather was a Portuguese admiral.

Albuquerque was given his education at the king's court, where he learned Latin and arithmetic and where he also became a friend of Prince John, the future King John II. With his family in such high standing, Albuquerque easily moved into the military service. He served the king on crusades in Northern Africa, where the Portuguese consistently strove to gain control from the Muslims.

Albuquerque was an impressive soldier and was given the post of "Master of the Horse" when his friend Prince John became King John II of Portugal in 1481.[21] He served his friend in that capacity until John's death in 1495.

---

[20] Podell, J. and Anzovin, S. *Old Worlds to New: The Age of Exploration and Discovery*. 1993.
[21] Stephens, H., *Albuquerque*. 2000.

In 1499, after Vasco da Gama returned to Portugal after sailing past the Cape of Good Hope to Asia, King John II's successor, King Manuel I, wasted no time in sending off another expedition.[22] This one had Pedro Álvares Cabral in charge of a mission to open up trade with India, even though there was a monopoly of Muslim traders there and the prince of Calicut had already rejected trading with Portugal. Even though Cochin (Kochi) was under the Zamorin, it did not reject Cabral's mission there.

Albuquerque arrived at Cochin in 1503.[23] He was sent by King Manuel to protect the leader of Cochin, who was supporting the Portuguese. To this end, Albuquerque and his men set about building a garrison at Cochin and a trading post at Kollam (Quilon). Once these were in place, and Cochin and its Portuguese interests were somewhat protected, Afonso de Albuquerque returned home to Lisbon in July of 1504.[24] King Manuel was pleased with his accomplishments and asked Albuquerque to take part in the work of making policies. He was then put in charge of a fleet of five ships, which would make up a larger group of sixteen under Tristão da Cunha.

This large fleet sailed for India in 1506. King Manuel I's goal for this mission was to build a fortress at Socotra, which would close off the trade route in the Red Sea to anyone but the Portuguese. By August of 1507, this mission had been accomplished, and Tristão da Cunha would part company with Albuquerque. Albuquerque had been given his own mission by the king, which was to take effect once he'd sailed as far as Mozambique.

Albuquerque was to take over Francisco de Almeida's position as the viceroy of India. Between the Persian Gulf and the Gulf of Oman,

---

[22] Velho, A., and de Sa, J., *A Journal of the First Voyage of Vasco Da Gama, 1497-1499.* 1898.

[23] Mathew, K.S., *Shipbuilding, Navigation and the Portuguese in Pre-modern India.* 2017.

Albuquerque took control of the island of Hormuz (Ormuz) and attempted to build a fortress there. When Albuquerque's captains disagreed with him and left him to sail on to India, his efforts to build the fortress had to be stopped. Albuquerque was left with only two ships, but he still continued to raid places along the Persian coast and the Arabian coast for Portugal.

In December of 1508, Albuquerque and his remaining ships finally arrived in India.[25] Almeida refused to give up his governing position to Albuquerque, regardless of the king's instructions. Almeida had successfully quashed Calicut's navy in 1509 but had then been attacked by Egypt, and in the fighting, Almeida's son had been killed.[26] Almeida was so adamant that he be allowed to exact his vengeance upon the Egyptians that he imprisoned Albuquerque to stop him from taking control. Almeida kept Albuquerque locked up until another Portuguese fleet arrived, after which he then stepped down from his position and handed control to his successor.

Afonso de Albuquerque continued his efforts to keep Portuguese control of the trade routes and also to build fortresses and keep them settled. In January of 1510, he tried to take Cochin but failed.[27] After that, he changed his strategy and sailed to Goa with 23 ships. Goa had long been held by Muslims, and Albuquerque decided attacking it would help strengthen the Portuguese presence in the area. So, in March of 1510, Albuquerque took control of Goa, although it only lasted until May, as he was forced out.[28] In November, he attacked again and was able to put down the Muslim defenses, and between six thousand and nine thousand of them died either in battle or from drowning in an attempt to escape.

From Goa, the Portuguese could establish powerful control over the spice trade route, as well as establish a base for their naval fleets.

[25] Stephens, H.M., *Rulers of India: Albuquerque.* 2019.
[26] Miller, Frederic P. et al. *Battle of Diu.* 2010.
[27] Ibid.
[28] Ibid.

The Hindu rulers did not challenge the Portuguese, and Albuquerque ensured that the government of Goa was taken care of before he set off to take control of Melaka (Malacca), which he did in July of 1511.[29] He returned to Goa in January 1512, though, as it was being attacked. He regained full control and once again left it to secure Portuguese control elsewhere. Albuquerque was unable to take Aden at the time, so he went on to investigate the Abyssinian coast and the Arabian coast. When he reached India, he finally took Calicut, which had been an enemy of the Portuguese expansion for a long time.

Albuquerque did finally gain control of part of the island of Hormuz, which he'd previously been unable to do. After the unsuccessful attempt in 1507, it became known that the king was under the control of his vizier, Reis Hamed, and lived in fear of him. In his 1515 meeting with the king, Albuquerque requested that the vizier also be present. He boldly had the man killed, which gave the king his freedom. After that, the Portuguese did not encounter resistance from Hormuz again.

In September of 1515, Albuquerque became ill.[30] In November, he set sail back to Goa, where he'd had much success. Because of Albuquerque, Goa held the first Portuguese mint in the East. The Hospital Real de Goa (Royal Hospital of Goa) was founded by Albuquerque as well. He'd admonished the doctors there once when he'd discovered they were overcharging the sick, and he tasked those doctors with the physical labor of building city walls to make them understand how the workers they treated came by their health problems.

An ill Albuquerque was to learn that he was to be replaced by a man he loathed. While he'd been busy securing Portugal's position, there were some speaking out against him to the king, including Lopo Soares de Albergaria, the man who was assigned to replace him. A

[29] Ibid.
[30] Brittanica.com

Portuguese fleet approached Albuquerque on his trip back to Goa, and the news reached Albuquerque, who became disillusioned but still managed to write a respectful final letter to King Manuel, as well as pen his last will and arrange for a council to manage the Portuguese state of India.

Albuquerque's ship was within sight of Goa when he died on December 16th, 1515.[31] The city mourned him deeply, and he was buried at Our Lady of the Hill Church, which he had built in 1513.

Some historians believe that if Albuquerque had lived longer, he would have been able to add the town of Aden into the Portuguese Empire. As it happened, his successor fumbled the transaction, declining the governor's offer to occupy and fortify the city in his eagerness to press onward and engage with the Egyptian fleet, a longtime Portuguese enemy. Upon returning to Aden after the military action had concluded, Lopo Soares found it had refortified itself and that the governor was in no mood to hand over authority to an outside power. The town was thus lost to Portugal.

---

[31] Ibid.

Chapter 5 – Christopher Columbus

Astonishingly little is known about the childhood and background of the man who would become world-famous for his voyage from Spain to the New World, although he was in search of India. Scholars cannot agree on his place of birth, though most believe it was Genoa, Italy, sometime in 1451.[32] Born to a Genoese wool merchant, Columbus struck out with his brother Bartholomew to become a sailor based in Portugal. The two found housing in Lisbon, as well as plenty of work in the busy port city.

The brothers found employment as mapmakers, but Christopher was eager to spend his time at sea. To that end, he became an entrepreneur within the Portuguese Merchant Marines. Sailing aboard commercial ships in 1477 and 1478, Columbus visited Ireland and Iceland, and he represented a Genoese company that needed him to purchase Portuguese sugar from Madeira.[33] The next year, he married Filipa Moniz Perestrelo, and in 1479 or 1480, their son Diego was

---

[32] "Christopher Columbus." *Encyclopedia Britannica.* Web.
[33] Ibid.

born.[34]

Most of the following years were spent at sea in the employ of the Portuguese Merchant Navy, which sent Columbus south along the western coast of Africa. It was during these years that Columbus learned the finer points of sailing the open seas, including the patterns of movement in the air. Filipa died in 1485, after which point Columbus took up a mistress by the name of Beatriz Enríquez de Arana of Córdoba.[35] Beatriz bore him a second son in 1488, whom they named Ferdinand.[36]

It was at some point after his first wife's passing that Columbus started ruminating on the possibility of crossing the entire Atlantic Ocean. Understanding that the world was a globe, he theorized that it was possible to travel west and eventually come upon the far eastern coast of China and India. He and others knew that it was in these Eastern countries that their most valuable items were made. If Columbus found a quicker route to the East, he could establish a firm trading route that benefited him and his patrons directly.

Unfortunately, King John II of Portugal was not intrigued enough to offer his sponsorship of the proposed voyage. After John's refusal, Columbus went to Spain to offer his loyalty to King Ferdinand II and Queen Isabella I instead. Firmly dedicated to his voyage, Columbus did not give up after the first two rejections he received from the Spanish monarchs. In fact, he continued to present his proposal for six years before Ferdinand and Isabella relented and finally offered him their patronage in January of 1492.

Permission was given for Columbus to undertake his Atlantic crossing most likely due to the changing political atmosphere at the time. Spain's king and queen were the Catholic power couple of Europe, and they were waging war on Spain's Islamic and Jewish communities. The final stronghold of the Islamic Moors fell at the

---

[34] Ibid.
[35] "Christopher Columbus." *Encyclopedia Britannica.* Web.
[36] Ibid.

Siege of Granada on January 2nd, 1492, and with this, Spain's confidence in its ability to erase non-Catholicism from the world increased dramatically.[37] The Ottoman Empire, however, stood in the way. If Columbus could indeed gain entry to the Eastern world via a western route, Ferdinand and Isabella could circumvent the Ottomans, replenishing Eastern trade and political influence.

Outfitted with three ships—the *Niña*, the *Pinta*, and the *Santa María*—Columbus set sail from the Spanish port of Palos on August 3rd, 1492.[38] Just over two months after heading west, Pero Gutierrez spied a vague point of light appearing sporadically in the distance and reported it to Columbus. The latter shouted at his crew to keep a careful lookout in that direction, and he was so concerned that they might miss a landmass that he promised a silk doublet and ten thousand *maravedís*—that is, Spanish copper coins—to the first man to spot land.[39] Rodrigo de Triana is credited with spotting the shore first, though Columbus took credit for the discovery and did not make good on his promise of payment.[40]

On October 12th, they made landfall on a small island that the natives called Guanahani. It was in the Bahamas, which the Spanish mistook for an island of the Indian Ocean. Not understanding that they had happened upon an entirely new continent, the crews explored a variety of islands there, including what would become Cuba, Haiti, and the Dominican Republic.

The following is an excerpt from Columbus' letter to Queen Isabella and King Ferdinand, detailing all he had found on these distant islands.

> As soon as we reached the island which I have just said was called Juana, I sailed along its coast some considerable

[37] Ibid.

[38] "Christopher Columbus Discovers America, 1492." *EyeWitness to History*. Web. 2004.

[39] Ibid.

[40] Nabhan, Gary Paul. *Cumin, Camels, and Caravans: A Spice Odyssey*. 2014.

distance towards the West, and found it to be so large, without any apparent end, that I believed it was not an island, but a continent, a province of Cathay. But I saw neither towns nor cities lying on the seaboard, only some villages and country farms, with whose inhabitants I could not get speech, because they fled as soon as they beheld us.

In all these islands, as I understand, every man is satisfied with only one wife, except the princes or kings, who are permitted to have 20. The women appear to work more than the men; but I could not well understand whether they have private property, or not; for I saw that what everyone had was shared with the others, especially meals, provisions and such things. I found among them no monsters, as very many expected; but men of great deference and kind; not are they black like Ethiopians; but they have long, straight hair.[41]

Columbus also noted the fact that the inhabitants of these islands had no guns and that their timid nature made him confident that a small Spanish army could conquer them easily. This piece of information did not go unnoticed. Furthermore, the spices, gold, brightly-colored birds, and tales of exotic naked people captured the imaginations of the Spanish monarchs, as well as at least two hundred investors.[42] The next voyage led by Columbus left Cádiz on September 24th, 1493, this time with at least seventeen ships.[43]

This time, the fleet was focused not only on finding stores of valuable trade items but also on implementing a Christian agenda and setting up colonies among the "Indians." A small cavalry accompanied the colonists, explorers, and sailors. When they once more disembarked at the fort they had constructed at La Navidad, it was clear that there had been violence between the Spanish and the Taíno

---

[41] "Columbus Reports his First Voyage." *The Gilder Lehrman Institute of American History.* 2012.
[42] "Christopher Columbus." *Encyclopedia Britannica.* Web.
[43] "Christopher Columbus." *Encyclopedia Britannica.* Web.

people, as all the Spanish were dead. Two men took it upon themselves to get revenge on the local people, capturing some of them to use as slaves. Forts were built in multitudes after this, and the first official Spanish settlement in the Americas was established at La Isabela on the northern coast of Hispaniola in 1494.[44]

The next two decades were characterized by violent clashes between the two ethnic groups, with members of the Taíno and other American tribes being captured and subjugated under the will of the Spanish conquistadors. Used to mine gold and serve the Spanish, the Taíno crops of yuca, sweet potatoes, and maize were neglected to the point that many of the indigenous people of the Caribbean starved. Others died due to infection from European diseases like smallpox until there were hardly any Taíno left at all, except those women who had been married off to conquistadors. A new culture and ethnicity emerged there, blended from Spanish conquistadors and settlers, native populations, and imported African slaves.

After Columbus' fleet left the islands they'd discovered, more Spanish and other Europeans flooded into the Americas, looking for ways to monetize this important discovery—though, for years, the Caribbean islands were still believed to belong to the eastern seas of China and India. This was the beginning of large-scale European colonization, warfare, and economic domination in what they would eventually realize was an unmapped continent.

---

[44] Poole, Robert M. "What became of the Taino?" *Smithsonian Magazine.* October 2011.

Chapter 6 – The Latter Voyages of Christopher Columbus

In 1498, Spanish monarchs Isabella and Ferdinand invested in a third Columbus-led expedition to the "East" composed of six ships. Half of these contained supplies for the Spanish settlement at Hispaniola, which was to be firmly fortified. Unfortunately, when the ships landed at Hispaniola, Columbus discovered extreme social unrest amongst both the enslaved Taíno and their Spanish lords. He sent a message to the king and queen of Spain, explaining that the colony was plagued by sickness, stubborn natives, and lazy Europeans.

Columbus had left his brothers Bartholomew and Diego in charge during his absence, but this seems to have been a mistake. Already, letters had been sent by the Spaniards at the settlement to the monarchy at home, and they rebelled alongside Francisco Roldán, the appointed mayor of La Isabella. Upon the return of Christopher Columbus, strict measures were used to get the people under control, and many people Columbus regarded as problematic were hanged.

Astonished at these accounts, Spain's king and queen sent a replacement for Columbus' governorship to the New World. This man, Francisco de Bobadilla, found that the Columbus brothers had exploited the Taínos by shipping them to Europe as slaves or forcing them to work in the gold mines. Under the original arrangement, the Taíno leaders were expected to produce gold on a per capita basis, but Diego and Bartholomew had modified that system and allowed certain Spaniards to control production directly. Not only did this anger the overworked miners, but it also infuriated those Spaniards who were not given such privileges.

Bobadilla found the Columbus brothers to have been the underlying problem in the colony, so he handcuffed them and sent them back to Spain aboard *La Gorda* in late October 1500.[45] During that journey, Christopher Columbus wrote a long and desperate letter to an important member of the Spanish court, Doña Juana de la Torre. Positioned as a nurse to Prince Juan, de la Torre had the ear of the sovereigns, and if she could be persuaded to have sympathy for Columbus, she might be able to convince Isabella and Ferdinand to free him.

Here is an excerpt from that letter:

> Though my complaint of the world is new, its habit of ill-using is very ancient. I have had a thousand struggles with it, and have thus far withstood them all, but now neither arms nor counsels avail me and it cruelly keeps me under water. Hope in the creator of all men sustains me; His help was always very ready; on another occasion, and not long ago, when I was still more overwhelmed, He raised me with his right arm, saying, O Man of little faith, arise, it is I; be not afraid.

> I came with so much cordial affection to serve these princes, and have served them with such service, as has never been heard of or seen.

> Of the new heaven and earth which our Lord made, when Saint John was writing Apocalypse, after what was spoken by the mouth of Isaiah, he made me the messenger, and showed

---

[45] "Christopher Columbus," *Encyclopedia Britannica*.

me where it lay. In all men there was disbelief, but to the Queen, my Lady, He gave the spirit of understanding, and great courage, and made her heiress of all, as a dear and much loved daughter. I went to take possession of all this in her royal name. They sought to make amends to her for the ignorance they had all shown by passing over their little knowledge and talking of obstacles and expenses. Her Highness, on the other hand, approved of it, and supported as far as she was able.

If I were to steal the Indies or the land which lies towards them of which I am now speaking, from the altar of Saint Peter, and give them to the Moors, they could not show greater enmity towards me in Spain...

Before my departure I many times begged their Highnesses to send there, at my expense, some one to take charge of the administration of justice; and after finding the Alcade in arms I renewed my supplications to have either some troops or at least some servant of theirs with letters patent; for my reputation is such that even if I build churches and hospitals, they will always be called dens of thieves...

They judge me over there as they would a Governor who had gone to Sicily, or to a city or town placed under regular government, and where the laws can be observed in their entirety without fear of ruining everything; and I am greatly injured thereby. I ought to be judged as a Captain who went from Spain to the Indies to conquer a numerous and warlike people, whose customs and religion are very contrary to ours; who live in rocks and mountains, without fixed settlements, and not like ourselves; and where, by the divine will, I have placed under the dominion of the King and Queen, our sovereigns, another world, through which Spain, which was reckoned a poor country, has become the richest.[46]

Indeed, Columbus and his brothers were quickly freed of their iron cuffs after landing in Spain, and Christopher gained an audience with the royals that December. Despite being unable to convince the monarchs that he was the best fit as governor of the new lands, Columbus was still considered the best navigator and admiral in Spain. Therefore, he was granted another voyage to the New World, under the assumption that there were yet new lands and valuables to be discovered in the name of Spain.

The next year, Isabella and Ferdinand sent Nicolás de Ovando westward with thirty ships to replace Bobadilla as the governor of the Indies.[47] In 1502, they also outfitted Columbus with ships and supplies with which to mount his fourth expedition to the west.[48] Columbus, however, received a relatively paltry four ships. During this time, the famous admiral began to see his discovery of unknown lands as his God-given fate and simultaneously seemed to believe that his hardships in governing those lands were akin to the suffering of Christ. He called himself "Christ-bearer," probably as a way to draw attention to these similarities and remind his investors that his ultimate mission was to spread Christianity to the people of the New World. He also began writing *Book of Prophecies* and *Book of Privileges*, the latter of which detailed the multitude of financial and title claims to which he and his heirs were privy.

Banned from embarking once more upon Hispaniola due to reports that he was an inept and vicious governor there, Columbus was instructed to continue explorations in the south and to find a passage to India. Though appearing outwardly to take these demands quite seriously, he appeared at Hispaniola that same June, calling

---

[46] Documented by Filson Young in *Christopher Columbus and the New World of his Discovery*. 2018.
[47] "Christopher Columbus," *Encyclopedia Britannica*.
[48] Ibid.

upon Governor Ovando to let him in. The governor refused outright, and only then did Columbus disappear further into uncharted waters.

During the summer months of 1502, Columbus found and partially explored the coasts of Jamaica, Cuba, Honduras, and Nicaragua.[49] Hoping to find a passage to India through the Chiriquí Lagoon in Panama, Columbus carefully sailed along the edge of the inlet before disembarking there to search for gold. His ships suffering from shipworm, and the admiral himself in poor health, Columbus nevertheless persisted into the depths of Panama during bad weather. In February of 1503, he even tried to set up a trading post in that part of the land, but when one ship was lost to disease and the native peoples showed no signs of cooperating, the plan was called off.[50] The remaining two ships were forced to return to Hispaniola. In too poor condition to make it that far, however, the crews beached both ships in Jamaica.

Captains Diego Méndez and Bartolomeo Fieschi headed toward Hispaniola by canoe to find help, paddling some 450 miles (720 kilometers) to reach Governor Ovando.[51] After having reached the colony, neither captain could convince the governor to send help quickly. The castaways in Jamaica waited nearly an entire year for rescue, after which Columbus sailed back to Spain to find that Queen Isabella was dying.

The queen, Columbus' main supporter and investor, died in late November 1504.[52] Her departure from the world meant not only could the aging Columbus no longer propose lavish expeditions to the west but also that his hopes of restoring his much-marred reputation were crushed. The adventurer did not long outlive his queen, dying in May 1506, but his voyages to what he fixedly called China and India—stoutly redressing those who supposed such lands were new to

---

[49] Ibid.
[50] "Christopher Columbus." *Encyclopedia Britannica.*
[51] Ibid.
[52] Potter, Philip J. *Queens of the Renaissance.* 2014.

European maps altogether—initiated an unprecedented flood of westward exploration and colonization.

Chapter 7 – Amerigo Vespucci

Though it was largely accepted by Europeans that Christopher Columbus was the first of their continent to discover the lands of the New World, there were some who disagreed. A group of unknown publishers printed a manuscript entitled *Mundus novus* in 1503 in which Amerigo Vespucci was named as the discoverer of the New World.[53] Vespucci, a gifted navigator from the Republic of Florence, traveled to Spain with a relative to work in the shipping industry. He was a member of the crew who prepared the ships for Columbus' second voyage.

Though Vespucci's first voyages were made under the authority of Spain, he sailed for the Portuguese after 1500. This switch seems most likely to have been due to Portugal's willingness to let Vespucci plan his expeditions freely, whereas Spain had begun to turn down his requests for funded expeditions. Always eager to have the best and most ambitious navigators working for their own goals, Portugal was happy to employ him.

Evidence of Vespucci's naval exploits can be found primarily in a selection of letters he sent to friends and acquaintances, including the perpetual gonfaloniere of the Republic of Florence, one Piero

---

[53] Drees, Clayton J. (editor.) *The Late Medieval Age of Crisis and Renewal.* 2001.

Soderini. The following is an excerpt of a 1504 letter to Soderini, outlining how Vespucci had found the main continent of a new world that challenged Columbus' interpretations of his own discoveries:

The principal reason why I am induced to write is the request of the bearer, Benvenuto Benvenuti, the devoted servant of your Excellency and my particular friend. He happened to be here in this city of Lisbon, and requested that I would impart to your Excellency a description of the things seen by me in various climes, in the course of the four voyages which I have made for the discovery of new lands, two by the authority and command of Don Ferdinand, King of Castile, in the great Western Ocean and the other two by order of Dom Manuel, King of Portugal, towards the south.

So I resolved to write, as requested, and set about the performance of my task, because I am certain that your Excellency counts me among the number of your most devoted servants, remembering that in the time of our youth, we were friends, going daily to study the rudiments of grammar, under the excellent instruction of the venerable brother of St. Mark, Friar Georgio Antonio Vespucci, my uncle, whose counsels would to God I had followed! For then, as Petrarch says, I should have been a different man from what I am.

...subject to very many inconveniences and dangers, I concluded to abandon mercantile affairs and direct my attention to something more laudable and stable. For this purpose, I prepared myself to visit various parts of the world, and see the wonderful things which might be found therein.

King Ferdinand of Castile had ordered four ships to go in search of new lands, and I was selected by his highness to go in that fleet, in order to assist in the discoveries. We sailed from the port of Cadiz on the 10th of May, 1497, and steering our course through the great Western Ocean, spent eighteen months in our expedition, discovering much land and a great number of islands, the largest part of which were inhabited. As these are not spoken of by the ancient writers, I presume they were ignorant of them. If I am not mistaken, I well remember to have read in one of their books, which I possessed, that this ocean was considered unpeopled.[54]

In another letter, Vespucci describes his second voyage to the southwest in 1499, during which he made even more discoveries:

We set out from the port of Cadiz, three ships in company, on the 18th of May, and steered directly for the Cape de Verdes, passing within sight of the Grand Canary, and soon arriving at an island called De Fuego, or Fire Island, whence, having taken wood and water, we proceeded on our voyage to the southwest. In forty-four days we arrived at a new land, which we judged to be a continent, and a continuation of that mentioned in my former voyage.[55]

It is believed by many historians that during this 1499 voyage, Vespucci was the first European to sail southward along the coast of Brazil and Venezuela. Unlike Christopher Columbus, Vespucci recognized that what he was seeing was not, in fact, part of China or India but an entirely new continent that did not exist on any European maps. This, he knew, was a new world. Ultimately, it was the fact that Amerigo Vespucci understood the relative relationship between Europe, the New World, and distant China, which solidified him, in many minds, as the true discoverer of the Americas. In fact, it is for him that the continents bear that name.

A pamphlet published by a humanist philosopher by the name of Martin Waldseemüller suggested that the New World take the name of the man who first realized its existence. This literature appeared in 1507, which was soon after the same publisher released "The Four

---

[54] Collection of letters and writings in *Amerigo Vespucci: Discover the man behind the legend.* 2017.
[55] Ibid.

Voyages of Amerigo." In the latter, a large star chart was included that laid out the navigational astronomy of South America. Across the continent, the name "Amerigo" was printed. Waldseemüller's suggestion proved quite popular, and soon the whole of South America was known as "Amerigo."

Vespucci's naval prowess and extreme rise in popularity impressed even Spain's King Ferdinand II, who gave Vespucci Spanish citizenship so that he could employ him once again. In 1508, Vespucci was made Master Navigator, a post in which he trained navigators and ship's pilots and revised existing maps. Even the maps drawn up by Christopher Columbus would have come to Vespucci for updates and changes. Christopher Columbus, however, remained certain that his own discoveries had revealed the eastern edge of Cathay, and he died believing this.

Chapter 8 – Ponce de León

Juan Ponce de León was born in Spain sometime between 1460 and 1474.[56] He was born into a noble family, and he served the royal court of Aragon as a page. He entered military service and fought in Granada against the Moors (Muslims), who were eventually expelled from Spain.

It is thought that Ponce de León may have been employed on Christopher Columbus' second expedition in 1493.[57] He is known to have settled on the island of Hispaniola, which is now the island that is split between the Dominican Republic and Haiti. He was married there in 1502, and the couple had four children.[58]

In Hispaniola, the Europeans, including Ponce de León, fought to take full control of the island from its native population. They made slaves of the native people and tried to take the land and turn it into European-style farms. Juan Ponce de León became governor of the eastern part of Hispaniola. This was a reward for his assistance earlier in the overtaking of the natives, and Ponce de León was also given land and slaves with which to set himself up as a farmer. Due to this

---

[56] Otfinoski, S. *Juan Ponce de Leon: Discoverer of Florida. 2005*
[57] Robinson, M.J. *Ponte Vedra Beach: A History.* 2008
[58] Robinson, M.J. *Ponte Vedra Beach: A History.* 2008

generous gift, his farming efforts were very successful.

Ponce de León sought more than farming success, however, and he was encouraged by the stories of gold on the nearby island called Borinquen. In 1508, Ponce de León received permission from the Spanish Crown to explore and colonize the island, which later became known as Puerto Rico.[59] It is thought that he may have actually done some exploring there already without official permission, and Ponce de León was made governor of Puerto Rico in 1509. The governorship of the island was disputed by the son of Christopher Columbus, however, on the grounds that Columbus had been granted that right first and that it should fall to his son upon his death. By 1511, the junior Columbus (Diego) was given the title after a legal decision was made, and Ponce de León was urged to further his explorations elsewhere.[60]

Ponce de León had grown rich on the plantations he'd built and from the mining operations he was involved in. Diego Columbus seized property from Ponce de León after his attempt to ignore the acknowledged right of Columbus to rule Puerto Rico. King Ferdinand II wanted Ponce de León to move on and explore more. He was possibly interested in finding the Fountain of Youth that was supposedly mentioned by the indigenous peoples of the Caribbean. The idea that Ponce de León and King Ferdinand II were seeking this mythical fountain is something that is often mentioned about them, but it remains unproven. One piece of remaining proof that there was talk of such a fountain can be found in a letter from a man named Peter Martyr, who was a contemporary of Ponce de León's. He wrote to the bishop of Rome, which said the following:

> Among the islands on the north side of Hispaniola [Haiti] there is one about three hundred and twenty-five leagues distant, as they say which have searched the same, in which is a

---

[59] Worth, Richard. *Puerto Rico: From Colony to Commonwealth.* 2016
[60] Otfinoski, S. *Juan Ponce de Leon: Discoverer of Florida.* 2005

continual spring of running water, of such marvelous virtue, that the water thereof being drunk perhaps with some diet, make the older men young again. And I here must make protestation to your holiness not to think this to be said lightly or rashly, for they have so spread this rumor for a truth throughout all the court, that not only all the people, but also many of them whom wisdom or fortune hath divided from the common sort, think it to be true.[61]

Other than this plea to the bishop to not allow such nonsense to be taken seriously, there is little evidence that Ponce de León and King Ferdinand II had their sights on such mythical treasures. They were, however, most definitely in search of new lands, such as the one they hoped to be Bimini—or the legendary Fountain of Youth—and other undiscovered lands that could add to the wealth of the kingdom.

King Ferdinand gave Ponce de León permission in February 1512 to further explore the Caribbean Sea.[62] Ponce de León set about preparing three ships and gathering a crew. On March 4th, 1513, they left Puerto Rico.[63] This expedition was the first European voyage to what would become known as Florida (Ponce de León named it La Florida). On April 3rd, 1513, the explorers came ashore on foot from their anchored ships.[64] During the expedition, Ponce de León traveled to the Florida Keys and to the Gulf Coast.

When he returned to Spain in 1514, King Ferdinand granted him a knighthood.[65] King Ferdinand also took this opportunity to give Ponce de León back his title as the governor of Puerto Rico and the as-yet-undiscovered Bimini, as well as permission to colonize Florida for Spain. Ponce de León sailed back to the Caribbean in 1515 to

---

[61] Davis, T.F. The Record of Ponce de Leon's Discovery of Florida, 1513. The Florida Historical Society Quarterly, Vol. 11, No. 1 (Jul., 1932)
[62] Ibid.
[63] Ibid.
[64] Ibid.
[65] Ibid.

prepare for another expedition to Florida but would soon find it necessary to first travel back to Spain, as King Ferdinand died on January 23rd, 1516.[66] Ponce de León went back to Spain after Ferdinand's death to ensure that the titles he'd been given and the grants he'd received would still be honored. After two years, Ponce de León had these affairs in order and headed back to Puerto Rico. His second expedition to Florida finally set off on February 20th, 1521.[67] This expedition took around two hundred men to the new land, as the settlement of a colony was planned. They also took horses, livestock, and farming implements to be used in the settling of the region.

This time, however, the Spaniards encountered very hostile defenses by the Calusa people, who were indigenous to Florida. The hopes of leaving a colony of settlers behind had to be abandoned. Juan Ponce de León himself was shot in the thigh with an arrow during an attack on the intruding colonists. It is believed the arrow was poisoned to cause illness. Ponce de León was taken to Havana, Cuba, but did not recover and died soon after. His body was taken home to his wife and family in Puerto Rico and interred there.

---

[66] Olson, J.S. *Historical Dictionary of European Imperialism.* 1991.
[67] Hamilton-Waxman, L. *A Journey with Juan Ponce de León.* 2018

Chapter 9 – Diogo Lopes de Sequeira

Don Diogo Lopes de Sequeira, born in 1465, was a Portuguese *fidalgo,* meaning that he was part of a noble family. [68] As such, Sequeira found work serving the Portuguese Empire as an explorer and diplomat. With Portugal spreading its wings rapidly, Sequeira found himself abroad as far from home as India, Malaysia, and Madagascar. In these places, he was tasked with investigating whether or not it would benefit Portugal to establish regular trade there. King Manuel I, the successor to his cousin King John II, also ordered Sequeira to compose a map of Madagascar and take the opportunity to learn more about the Chinese, who were likely to be found in that part of the world.

In King Manuel's letter of instruction to Diogo Lopes de Sequeira in February of 1508, he insisted that no one among the expedition should undertake any acts of war or hostility:

> We order and command that you should do no damage or harm at all parts you reach, and rather that all should receive honour, favour, hospitality and fair trade from you, for our

---

[68] Chen, Li. *Chinese Law in Imperial Eyes.* 2015.

service so demands it in these beginnings. And though something may be committed against you in your venture, and you might be in you right to cause harm, dissimulate it as best you can, showing that you wish not but peace and friendship, for we demand it of you. However should you be attacked, or deceived in such a manner that it may seem to you that they wished to do you harm, then you shall do all damage and harm as you can to those who sought to commit it against you, and in no other situation shall you do war or harm.

Sequeira embarked on a hugely important voyage, one that would truly solidify Portugal's presence, influence, and authority in places few Europeans had ever seen. With sixteen ships, Sequeira's journey began in 1508, starting southward from Lisbon and sailing along the Cape of Good Hope.[69] In the southern part of Africa, the ships anchored at St. Bras and took in a supply of fresh water. From there, they proceeded to Mozambique and then Madagascar.

The previous year, Pero d'Arraya had embarked upon Mozambique's chief port, Sofala, with six ships.[70] There, he was to found a fortress and begin the colonization of the island country. With the permission of a local lord to go ahead and build, d'Arraya erected a stronghold for Portugal, filling it with arms and ammunition. When the local people realized it had not been d'Arraya's intention to live simply and peacefully among them, they banded together to try to force the Portuguese back out of Mozambique.

Local efforts failed, and when the Portuguese killed the people's ruler, d'Arraya went ahead and appointed the next one. Ongoing strife, political reorganization, and violence ultimately left the fortress at Sofala very low on inhabitants. By the time Diogo Lopes de Sequeira reached Mozambique, there was little he or anyone could do to secure the area, let alone increase the population of the seriously

---

[69] McMurdo, Edward. *The History of Portugal.* 1889.
[70] Ibid.

waning colony. He inspected the conditions there and soon moved on to Madagascar.

It was in August of 1508, while they were moored in the Bay of St. Sebastian and exploring the island of Madagascar, when Sequeira and fellow captain Duarte de Lemos rescued three stranded sailors who had been victims of an earlier Portuguese shipwreck.[71] One of the sailors, named Antonio, had learned the local Malagasy language and afterward served as an interpreter for Sequeira. Antonio went with his rescuer and the accompanying ships to their most important destination: Malacca, located in modern-day Malaysia.

They arrived in the city of Malacca in September of 1509.[72] Sequeira brought with him a letter from the Portuguese king, Manuel I. The letter was a customary one, designed to introduce local leaders and merchants to the far-off country of Portugal and request friendly trading relationship between the two nations.

Malacca was a large and bustling international trading city, whose fame had reached the ears of European explorers and monarchs long before their ships made port. Established as the capital city of the Malacca Sultanate around the year 1400, it was comprised of a dynamic population that included members of several denominations, including Islam, Buddhism, and Taoism.[73] Flowing with people who spoke Mandarin, Arabic, Javanese, Persian, and Japanese, the Malacca Sultanate was maintained by the skillful military might of many formal knights who spoke up to a dozen languages.

On the same day that Diogo Lopes de Sequeira's ship made port in Malacca, the Portuguese captain was introduced to four Chinese captains in charge of junk ships. Unused to the variety of customs and ethnicities found in Malacca, Sequeira believed his new friends were from some other part of Europe. Regardless of their obvious faults in communicating, the Portuguese and Chinese captains dined regularly

---

[71] Van den Boogaerde, Pierre. *Shipwrecks of Madagascar.* 2011.
[72] Ibid.
[73] Cœdès, George. *The Indianized states of Southeast Asia.* 1968.

together on one another's ships. Unfortunately, a faction of the local Muslim population was not so friendly.

Muslim explorers were already somewhat familiar with the Portuguese from their presence in India, and they warned others against beginning trade or political relations with Sequeira. Despite having made friendships with many people in Malacca, Sequeira was made the object of an assassination plot. Hearing about the plan just in time to save his own life, Sequeira fled the city on one of his ships, leaving several of his own crew members behind. He made it back to Lisbon in 1510.[74]

In 1518, Diogo Lopes de Sequeira was named the governor of India, replacing Lopo Soares de Albergaria.[75]

---

[74] McMurdo, Edward. *The History of Portugal.* 1889.
[75] Benians, Ernest Alfred; Arthur Percival Newton and John Holland Rose (editors.) *The Cambridge History of the British Empire.* 1940.

Chapter 10 – Hernán Cortés

Hernán Cortés (originally known as Hernando or Fernando Cortez) was born in 1485 in Spain.[76] His father was a captain in the Spanish army, and his mother was a cousin to Francisco Pizarro, who conquered the Incan Empire in what would become known as Peru. Cortés was not well as a child. When he was fourteen years old, he began to study law with an uncle so that he would be able to have a career despite his sickly ways. By sixteen, Cortés returned to his parents in Medellín and was well educated in law, but he had an arrogant attitude and considered his home too provincial and backward for someone such as himself.

By this time, Spain was receiving the full glory of the successes of Christopher Columbus, and Cortés was drawn to the world of exploration. Cortés was distantly related to Nicolás de Ovando, who had been appointed as the governor of Hispaniola (the island that is now the Dominican Republic and Haiti), and the family organized for Cortés to travel there. He didn't leave right away, however, as he received an injury and spent the next year in the southern ports of Spain. In 1504, Cortés finally left for Hispaniola on Alonso

---

[76] Savage, C. *Illustrated Biography: Or, Memoirs of the Great and the Good of All Nations*. 1853.

Quintero's ship.[77]

It is thought that Quintero's behavior influenced Cortés during the voyage. Quintero was a conquistador with his eye on whatever advantage he could take. He was mutinous and rather devious.

When he reached Hispaniola at the age of eighteen, Cortés settled into life in the colony very well as a farmer. When registering as a citizen there, he received land with which to farm and build a home. He was appointed as a notary for the town of Azua de Compostela, and the governor gave him an *encomienda*, a group of native slave laborers, as a reward.

Cortés began looking at joining expeditions to Cuba, and in an odd turn of luck, he became ill with syphilis, which caused him to miss his chance to sail with Diego de Nicuesa and Alonso de Ojeda when they sailed in 1509.[78] Nicuesa's fate was to be put out to sea after being denied entry at Santa Maria after he discovered it had already been settled by Vasco Núñez de Balboa. Nicuesa intended to punish those already there, but instead, he and seventeen of his most loyal followers were sent away. The rest of the men on his voyage were granted entry. Nicuesa set off to return to Santo Domingo but was never seen again. Alonso de Ojeda ended up shipwrecked and was lucky to be rescued, but that would be his last expedition.

And so, Cortés recovered from his illness and sailed in 1511 with Diego Velázquez de Cuéllar to Cuba.[79] Velázquez was to be the governor once there and Cortés the treasury clerk. Along with his new position in Santiago, Cuba, Cortés was given land and slaves, who were from the native population. As he settled into his new role, which gave him some power in the area, he and Velázquez began to disagree on many things, and Cortés had the ear of those in the colony who were dissatisfied. By 1514, he was at the head of a group

[77] Bjorklund, L. *A Brief History of Fairplay*. 2013.
[78] Bancroft, H.H. *The Works of Hubert Howe Bancroft*. 1883
[79] Tarver, H.M. and Slape, E. *The Spanish Empire: A Historical Encyclopedia*. 2016.

that was making demands for more slaves to be provided to the settlers by the governing body.[80] Cortés came to be elected as *alcalde* (mayor) in Santiago in two elections.

By October of 1518, Velázquez decided to send Cortés to aid his relative Juan de Grijalva in Mexico, where they had discovered considerable amounts of gold and silver. Cortés was given the title of Captain-General for this expedition. Velázquez later changed his mind about placing Cortés in charge as their rivalry increased when Cortés was able to engage several ships and hundreds of men for the voyage in a short amount of time. Cortés ignored the cancellation, and with eleven ships, sixteen horses, and five hundred men he'd engaged from different ports of Cuba, he set sail for Mexico in February of 1519.[81]

Cortés' expedition reached Tabasco the following month in March of 1519.[82] They anchored there for a while before moving on. While there, Cortés was able to gain the friendship of the natives. From Tabasco, Cortés sailed to (and founded) Veracruz, where he became the chief justice and his men became the citizens of the newly founded colony. In a move to solidify his rule and the settlers' commitment to the new colony, he took away their ability to leave by destroying all the ships.

While many of the native peoples were treated fairly and became friends of Cortés, there were many who did not, and he was quick to attack with force rather than negotiate. The Tlaxcalan and Cholula people became the enemies of Cortés in his quest to take control of the Aztec Empire. In 1521, Cortés marched to Tenochtitlán, the seat of the Aztec Empire (now Mexico City), which was where their ruler, Montezuma II, reigned.[83]

As was the usual custom, Montezuma welcomed Cortés as a visitor. Cortés did not return the cordial treatment, however, and decided to

---

[80] Malveaux, E. *The Color Line: A History*. 2015.
[81] Honychurch, L. *Caribbean People*. 1995.
[82] Ibid.
[83] Ibid.

take Montezuma as a hostage in order to force the Aztecs to accept the religious and political conversions the Spanish insisted upon. At first, Cortés insisted to Montezuma that he was keeping him safe, but, of course, it was actually a kidnapping. Cortés allowed his soldiers to plunder the city. A contributing factor to the demise of the Aztec was that they fell ill to smallpox in large numbers. They had no immunity to this disease from Europe. By 1521, the Aztec Empire had become a power of the past, and the Spanish conquistadors had begun the transformation of their land into an extension of Spain. In October 1522, Charles V, the Holy Roman emperor and the king of Spain, among many other titles, made Cortés the captain-general of New Spain.[84]

Hernán Cortés took charge and began work in Mexico City to build up the city as part of the Spanish Empire. In doing so, the destroying of the work of the Aztecs was undertaken, and the old temples and buildings were ruined.

Diego Velázquez de Cuéllar continued in his effort to cause interference for Cortés and wrote to his friend Bishop Fonseca in Spain, who campaigned against Cortés, and the Spanish Crown sent Francisco de Garay to settle northern Mexico. Cortés wrote to the king himself, and a decree was sent by Charles V for de Garay to abandon his mission there.

Only two years after becoming Captain-General of New Spain, Cortés began looking again at an expedition of exploration. In 1524, he went into the jungle of Honduras.[85] His political power began to cause concern in Spain when he took on Cristóbal de Olid, who had already claimed Honduras. He'd also taken Cuauhtémoc, the last independent Aztec leader, and some other native people of rank along with him when he went to Honduras because he was afraid to leave them behind in Mexico for fear they'd revolt while he was away.

---

[84] Pohl, J. *The Conquistador: 1492–1550.* 2012.
[85] Ibid.

When Cuauhtémoc ended up being killed by Cortés, as well as when Cortés issued his own decree for the death of Olid, the Council of Indies and the Crown of Castile distanced themselves from Cortés and his actions.

Velázquez and Bishop Fonseca, in their continued efforts to see Cortés lose his power, finally convinced the king to appoint someone to investigate Cortés and his activities. Luis Ponce de León was tasked with the job, and when Cortés returned from Honduras, he was suspended from his political office. When Luis Ponce de León died very soon after his arrival, Cortés was suspected by many of poisoning him, but he did not take control of the office again. Alonso de Estrada became governor of New Spain in 1527, while Cortés retired to his estate.[86]

Cortés sailed back to Spain in 1528 in order to convince the king to allow him to retake his position, taking treasures from New Spain with him for the monarch. Charles V allowed Cortés to maintain the title of Captain-General but did not agree to reinstate him as governor. In 1530, Cortés sailed for the last time to New Spain, where he spent some time reasserting his power and putting the colony back in order, as well as dealing with accusations that he'd murdered his first wife. He remarried and settled at his estate, which was south of Mexico City.

Cortés continued to explore, and in 1536, he found the Baja California Peninsula and explored the Mexican coast on the Pacific side. In 1539, Francisco de Ulloa named the Sea of Cortez in honor of Hernán Cortés. It was later called the Gulf of California.[87]

In 1541, Cortés sailed one last time to Spain.[88] He had many lawsuits against him and was disheartened by what he considered a

---

[86] Valencia, R.H. *The Encomenderos of New Spain, 1521-1555*. 2009.
[87] Francisco López de Gómara, *Cortes: The Life of the Conqueror by his Secretary*. 1964.
[88] Kohl, J.G. *A Popular History of the Discovery of America from Columbus to Franklin*. 1865.

lack of recognition. He died on December 2nd, 1547, without ever returning to Mexico again.[89]

---

[89] Ibid.

Chapter 11 – Ferdinand Magellan

Ferdinand Magellan (Fernão de Magalhães) was born around 1480 into Portuguese nobility, and under the reign of King John II, Magellan served as a page boy to John II's wife, Queen Eleanor.[90]

In 1505, with the country now under the rule of King Manuel I, Magellan signed up to serve on a fleet headed to the African and Indian coasts. This fleet was to continue Portugal's vigilant efforts in keeping the presence of Portugal visible to all, especially the Muslims, who the Portuguese were in a constant state of rivalry over trade access. This expedition was headed by Francisco de Almeida, who had been appointed as viceroy of Portuguese India.

Magellan's sailing experiences would come to have more warring activity than many of the previous Portuguese expeditions, which were mostly exploratory in nature and did not deal much with fighting for trade supremacy.

In February of 1509, Magellan was to take part in a naval battle in the Arabian Sea near the port of Diu, India.[91] The Portuguese exerted

---

[90] Zweig, S. *Magellan: Conqueror of the Seas.* 2019.
[91] Brittanica.com

their efforts against their Muslim rivals, which consisted of the Kingdom of Calicut, the Mamluk Sultanate, and the Gujarat Sultanate. Calicut had been a foe of Portugal from the start when Vasco da Gama had arrived there and tried to secure a trade agreement. This battle lasted for three days, and in the end, the Portuguese were victorious. Their win here gave them naval supremacy over the majority of the Indian Ocean, which meant their trading efforts could proceed.

In 1511, Magellan was part of General Afonso de Albuquerque's expedition to Malacca.[92] Malacca was a coastal city that had yet to come under Portuguese control and was, therefore, a target for total trade control of the area. Albuquerque's fleet of 22 ships was successful in defeating Malacca, but it took them six weeks to do so. This victory was a major one for Portugal, which now held the Malacca Strait and controlled access to the Malaysian ports. The Capture of Malacca was yet another victory for Portugal, and Magellan was given a promotion and rewarded with goods that had been plundered from the conflict.

In 1513, Magellan went on an expedition from Lisbon led by James, Duke of Braganza.[93] This fleet was heading to Azamor (Azemmour), which was under the control of the Moroccans. King Manuel I of Portugal sent the fleet in response to Governor Moulay Zayam's refusal to pay Portugal the vassalage fees they'd been paying since 1486. On September 1ˢᵗ, 1513, the Portuguese took the city with no resistance from the Moroccans.

Magellan fell out of favor with King Manuel I at some point. He'd received a leg injury and had taken leave from service without having sought permission. Beyond that, Magellan had repeatedly requested increased rewards or pensions from the king, who had refused any increase. Magellan was also rumored to have sold some of the war

---

[92] Ibid.
[93] Infobase Publishing, *Ferdinand Magellan -Facts On File*. 2009.

plunder back to the enemies of Portugal after they took Azamor. Magellan sought the king's backing for an expedition to the Spice Islands but was refused this as well.

Magellan left Portugal and traveled to Spain, where, along with the Portuguese cosmographer Rui Faleiro, went to Valladolid to seek an audience with King Charles I of Spain, who would later become the Holy Roman emperor. The two offered to sail west of the Cape Verde Islands, which belonged to Portugal, to prove that the Spice Islands were actually a part of the Spanish-owned territories rather than the Portuguese. They also proposed a fruitful trade route for Spain. There had been a theory among some that finding a passage through the west meant that the Spanish could reach their destination without dealing with the Portuguese at the Cape of Good Hope. Magellan's proposal, if successful, would mean an entirely Spanish route for trade, which could even add new lands that might be discovered along the way. Unlike King Manuel I of Portugal, the young King Charles I of Spain was agreeable. He gave Magellan his approval on March 22nd, 1518, and he agreed to provide most of the funding needed for the expedition.[94]

There were many who were not pleased with Magellan's new expedition. Firstly, many in Spain argued against such an important mission being given to a non-Spaniard. Magellan encountered difficulties in preparing his voyage when Juan Rodríguez de Fonseca, who was in charge of Spain's House of Commerce, attempted to withhold services. This caused delays for the expedition and, in the end, caused Magellan to lose his chosen Portuguese co-captain Faleiro. Fonseca replaced the co-captain with his own choice of a Spanish officer.

Five ships manned by around 270 men, mostly Spanish and Portuguese, made up Magellan's fleet. They took enough supplies with them to travel for two years. The ships making the trip were the

---

[94] Aretha, D., *Magellan: First to Circle the Globe*. 2009.

Trinidad, which was the flagship, the *San Antonio*, the *Concepcion*, the *Victoria*, and the *Santiago*. The ships were readied in Sevilla, where Magellan had married the daughter of a Sevillian official in 1517.[95] The ships were not what Magellan would have chosen for his expedition, but they were what he was given. They were not in top condition and were older than he liked.

By September 20th, 1519, though, the ships and the expedition were finally ready to go, and they sailed from Sanlúcar de Barrameda. They sailed to the Canary Islands and arrived on Tenerife by September 26th, 1519, where they rested for a few days before heading out toward Brazil on October 3rd, 1519.[96] Although they encountered some storms, they sailed past the equator and crossed the Atlantic with no losses. They arrived in Rio de Janeiro in Brazil on December 13th, 1519.[97]

Magellan led the expedition on and attempted to locate the strait they sought for their trade route. By March 31st, 1520, the ships were at Port St. Julian in Argentina. The Spaniard captains, Juan de Cartagena, Gaspar de Quesada, and Luis Mendoza, attempted to lead a mutiny against Magellan but were unsuccessful as Magellan was able to manage a resolution. In doing so, he forced Cartagena off his ship onto shore to remain there and beheaded Quesada. Mendoza had been killed in the attempted mutiny. The others involved were put into chains and given hard labor. With the fleet under control again, Magellan sailed from St. Julian on August 24th, 1520.[98]

The *Santiago* succumbed to a storm over the winter, but thankfully, no men were lost. The remaining ships kept up their search for the route to the Pacific Ocean, and they eventually found a strait that provided such passage. Magellan named it the Strait of All Saints because they sailed into it on All Saints' Day (November 1st). It would

[95] "Ferdinand Magellan." *Encyclopedia Britannica.*
[96] Oliveira, Fernão, The Voyage of Ferdinand Magellan. 2002.
[97] Ibid.
[98] Ibid.

later be renamed the Strait of Magellan. Another ship, the *San Antonio*, was lost to the fleet during the exploration of this strait when its crew deserted the expedition and headed back home to Spain. Unfortunately, the crew of the *San Antonio* took many of the supplies the other ships were counting on. The remaining ships, however, continued on, and later in November, they were in the Pacific Ocean, which was named by Magellan.

Since sailing in this area was new, Magellan did not realize the trip to Asia would be so far, as it would take them over three months to make the journey rather than the mere days he expected. Because of this, the fleet suffered depleted food and water, and around thirty men died from scurvy before they finally reached Guam on March 6th, 1521.[99] Unfortunately, the natives there were not receptive to the newcomers. They boarded their ships and took what they wanted. Magellan responded by sending men onto the island to retaliate and retake their goods.

The ships received a better reception when they arrived in the Philippines on March 16th, 1520. Not only could they rest and restock their food, but Magellan also made a friend of the leaders of the island of Limasawa and began to promote Christianity. Within two weeks, they'd put up a cross and started converting the natives. On April 21st, 1520, when Magellan's men tried to forcefully take charge of the island of Mactan, whose native population was resistant to conversion, they found the inhabitants were prepared to fight rather than accept this foreign religion.[100] Not only did these Europeans lose this aggressive attempt to take charge, but Magellan himself was also killed in the fight.

The fleet, which would be led by a succession of men on its way home, would leave the Philippines and reach Moluccas (Maluku) in November 1521.[101] They tried to leave for Spain in December, but

---

[99] Ibid.
[100] Zweig, S., Magellan: Conqueror of the Seas. 2019.
[101] Kurniawan, Y. *The Politics of Securitization in Democratic Indonesia*. 2017.

only one of the remaining two ships was actually seaworthy at this point, and so, the *Victoria* was the only ship left of the expedition as it finally set sail home. It reached Spain on September 6th, 1522, nearly four years after the expedition had begun. Less than twenty men were left of the crew.[102]

---

[102] Levinson, N. *Magellan and the First Voyage Around the World.* 2001.

Chapter 12 – John Cabot

John Cabot (Giovanni Caboto) was born in Italy around 1450.[103] He moved to Venice as early as 1461 and became a citizen there by 1476, which meant he agreed to spend at least fifteen years in the city.[104] He was often sent to the large trading centers of the Mediterranean in his work for a mercantile enterprise. Thus, he learned navigation and gained skills and techniques that would serve him later in exploration.

There are records indicating Cabot was involved in the building of houses in Venice. Cabot was not successful in his finances, though, and after becoming heavily in debt, he left Venice by 1488 and moved to Spain. There, he made a proposal to the city to improve their harbor, but they did not accept it. He then moved to Seville, Spain, in 1494. He made a proposal to the city there to construct a bridge. This time, he got the contract and worked at the construction project for five months before it was canceled. After this, Cabot began to look for support for an ocean expedition to the New World, and he moved his family to England the next year.[105] He received authorization from King Henry VII to make a voyage of exploration. By this time,

---

[103] Roberts, S., *John Cabot.* 2013.
[104] "John Cabot." *Encyclopedia Britannica.*
[105] Hunter, D., *Race to the New World.* 2012.

Christopher Columbus' discoveries had been reported, and Cabot offered a chance for Britain to be a part of the rush to discover new places. Cabot was to return to Bristol with goods from whatever new place he found and set up a trade monopoly. The king's letter to Cabot stated:

> Full and free authority, faculty and power to sail to all parts, regions and coasts of the eastern, western and northern sea, under our banners, flags and ensigns, with five ships or vessels of whatsoever burden and quality they may be, and with so many and with such mariners and men as they may wish to take with them in the said ships, at their own proper costs and charges, to find, discover and investigate whatsoever islands, countries, regions or provinces of heathens and infidels, in whatsoever part of the world placed, which before this time were unknown to all Christians.[106]

Cabot left Bristol in 1496 with one ship.[107] However, his voyage was not successful, and he turned back to England early on due to bad weather, a shortage of food supplies, and disagreements with his crew. Cabot regrouped and set off again in May of 1497, again with only one ship and a small crew of eighteen men.[108] They sailed across the ocean, and on June 24th, 1497, John Cabot reached what is now Canada.[109] It isn't clear exactly where he first landed, and there is debate as to whether it was Labrador, Newfoundland, Cape Breton Island, or even Nova Scotia. His landing was reported in the chronicle of Bristol:

> This year, on St. John the Baptist's Day [June 24th, 1497], the land of America was found by the Merchants of Bristow in a shippe of Bristowe, called the Mathew; the which said the ship departed from the port of Bristowe, the second day of

---

[106] Childs, D., Tudor Sea Power: The Foundation of Greatness. 2009.
[107] Archibald, M., *Across the Pond: Chapters from the Atlantic*. 2000.
[108] Ibid.
[109] Britannica Student Encyclopedia, 2014.

May, and came home again the 6th of August next following.[110]

Cabot claimed this land for England's King Henry VII, and he placed both the flag of England and the flag of Venice there in reverence of his citizenship. Cabot and his men noted that the area seemed to be inhabited, but they themselves did not meet any people. They continued along the coast, and Cabot gave names to the places they noted. Although his map of these places may not align with modern maps, they were in the general area of what is now known as Cabot Strait, located between Newfoundland and Cape Breton Island. These locations probably included what would come to be known as **Cape North, St. Paul Island, Cape Ray, St. Pierre and Miquelon, and Cape Race.** Cabot and his men did most of their exploring aboard their ship, and many of their discoveries took place after they'd turned around to sail back.

After Cabot returned to Bristol on August 6th, 1497, Cabot traveled to London to report directly to King Henry VII.[111] He explained what he'd discovered, and based on his time in the New World, he reported that the weather was temperate and there was good land to be found. He said that the fish were so plentiful that England would no longer require fish from Iceland with this new bountiful harvest at their disposal. As with the other explorers who first reached North America, he, too, believed he'd sailed to East India and proposed that for his second voyage, he would sail beyond his first landing place and come to Japan.

Cabot was given a new authorization from the king on February 3rd, 1498, and was soon off on his second voyage.[112] It is believed he had up to five ships and two hundred men for this second expedition, as well as fabrics to trade. It isn't known exactly what happened to Cabot's ships, but it is believed that they encountered a terrible storm.

[110] McNeill-Ritchie, S. *Historic England: Bristol: Unique Images from the Archives of Historic England.* 2018
[111] Schwartz, S., *Putting" America" on the Map.* 2007.
[112] Potter, P., *Explorers and Their Quest for North America.* 2018.

There is evidence that one of the ships made it to Ireland. With no word on Cabot, he was presumed to have died at sea by 1499.[113] Cabot's first voyage, however, was what began England's claim to North American lands.

---

[113] Anderson, Z., *John Cabot: Searching for a Westward Passage to Asia.* 2004.

Chapter 13 – The Laws of Burgos

The Laws of Burgos were issued by King Ferdinand II of Aragon in 1513 as a way to control the often violent and exploitative behavior of Spaniards on the other side of the Atlantic Ocean. It is believed that the creation of these laws is the legacy of Fray (Friar) Antonio de Montesinos, who delivered his first sermon on December 21st, 1511 (aka "the Christmas sermon"), advocating justice for the native peoples.[114] The issuance of these laws was intended for the island of Hispaniola, which comprises the modern nations of the Dominican Republic and Haiti.

The following is an excerpt from the formal legislation of the Burgos Laws:

> Whereas, it has become evident through long experience that nothing has sufficed to bring the said chiefs and Indians to a knowledge of our Faith (necessary for their salvation), since by nature they are inclined to idleness and vice, and have no manner of virtue or doctrine (by which Our Lord is disserved), and that the principal obstacle in the way of correcting their vices and having them profit by and impressing them with a doctrine is that their dwellings are remote from the settlements of the Spaniards who go hence to reside in the said Island, because, although at the time the Indians go to serve them they are indoctrinated in and taught the things of our Faith, after serving they return to their dwellings where, because of the distance and their own evil inclinations, they immediately forget what they have been taught and go back to their customary idleness and vice, and when they come to serve again they are as new in the doctrine as they were at the beginning, because although the Spaniard who accompanies them to their village, as is there ordered, reminds them of it

---

[114] Pastro, Vincent J. *Enflamed by the Sacramental World.* 2010.

---

and reprehends them, they, having no fear of him, do not profit by it and tell him to leave them in idleness, since that is their reason for returning to their said village, and that their only purpose and desire is to do with themselves what they will, without regard for any virtue, and,

Whereas, this is contrary to our Faith, and, since it is our determination to remove the said Indians and have them dwell near the Spaniards, we order and command that the persons to whom the said Indians are given, or shall be given, in encomienda, shall at once and forthwith build, for every fifty Indians, four lodges [bohíos] of thirty by fifteen feet, and have the Indians plant 5,000 hillocks (3,000 in cassava and 2,000 in yams), 250 pepper plants, and 50 cotton plants, and so on in like manner, increasing or decreasing the amount according to the number of Indians they have in encomienda, and these shall be settled next to the estates of the Spaniards who have them in encomienda, well situated and housed, and under the eyes of you, our said Admiral [Diego Columbus, son of Christopher Columbus] and judges and officers, and of our visitor who will be in charge of it, or of the person whom you, our said Admiral and judges and officers, shall send for the aforesaid purpose, and he, I charge and command you, shall be such as will be competent in this matter.

After the aforesaid has been done, we order and command that all the chiefs and Indians dwelling on the Island of Española, now or in the future, shall be brought from their present dwelling places to the villages and communities of the Spaniards who reside, now or in the future, on the said Island;

Also, we order and command that within two years [of publication of this ordinance] the men and women shall go about clad.

Given in the City of Valladolid, July 28, 1513.[115]

It was the intention of King Ferdinand II of Aragon to ensure two things. First, he wanted to make sure the indigenous peoples of the New World were treated in what he considered a humane manner, and secondly, he wanted to ensure that these same people were engaged in what he considered a reasonable portion of work. The natives, seemingly used to their own system of work and rest, were generally opposed to working long hours in the mines or performing rudimentary tasks for the Spaniards, who had captured or "purchased" them. To solve myriad problems in the colonies, Ferdinand declared that the native peoples be housed, clothed, and worked on a schedule. They were expected to plant gardens for themselves, for which the Laws of Burgos had very specific requirements.

Essentially, the passing of these laws over the people of Hispaniola politically doomed them to never return to the way of life they were born into. For Spain, however, it surely seemed the most responsible and charitable of actions. Though many of the laws were indeed followed, the legislation did not put a stop to economic exploitation and physical violence against the Native Americans.

---

[115] "1512-1513, Laws of Burgos." Taken from
http://faculty.smu.edu/bakewell/BAKEWELL/texts/burgoslaws.html.

Chapter 14 – Jacques Cartier

Jacques Cartier was a French explorer born in 1491 in Brittany.[116] Cartier became a mariner, and his early career is believed to have consisted mostly of sailing along the French coast, as well as to Brazil as a general sailor before being promoted to an officer. In 1520, he married into a prominent French family when he took Mary Catherine des Granches as his wife.[117] These family connections played a role in his ascent into the favor of King Francis I, who put him at the head of the expeditions he would come to be known for. In 1532, Brittany and France entered a union, and the politics of the day made Cartier a favorable choice by King Francis I to head the explorations after Giovanni da Verrazano, an Italian in service of France, died.[118]

In 1534, Jacques Cartier set sail on his first voyage as the man in charge. He was in search of a passage to Asia by either going around or through the New World (then called the northern lands) somehow. Of course, as with all the other explorations, gold, spices, and other valuables were expected to be found along the way.

---

[116] Greene, M. *Jacques Cartier: Navigating the St. Lawrence River.* 2004.
[117] Stein, S. *The Sea in World History.* 2017.
[118] Wilson, Neil. *Brittany.* 2002.

Cartier's expedition set off on April 20th, 1534, from Saint-Malo, France.[119] He had two ships and 61 men in his charge. Twenty days later, Cartier and his men reached the shores of what would become known as Canada. They sailed up to what is now Newfoundland and then sailed north to explore before exploring the coast going south. Along the west coast of Newfoundland, Cartier discovered Prince Edward Island, and he even sailed down the Gulf of Saint Lawrence to its outlet at Île d'Anticosti (Anticosti Island).

Cartier encountered some locals and did some small trading during this voyage. On July 24th, 1534, he erected a cross on the south shore of the Saint Lawrence River at Gaspé to claim the land for the king of France.[120] The Iroquois he encountered there did not appreciate his land claim, and when he captured two of Donnacona's sons, who was their chief, tensions developed. The Iroquois leader finally agreed to allow Cartier to take his sons but only on the condition that he returned with trade goods.

Cartier took his two captured men and headed back to France, where he safely returned on September 5th, 1534.[121] He called these men "Indians" because he thought he had reached Asia on his voyage. He called the new land he'd found Kanata, which is where the name Canada likely comes from, as the native men explained that "kanata" was what they called a settlement.

The king was indeed impressed by Cartier's report of what he'd found in the northern lands, and he immediately put him in charge of a second voyage to explore the new lands further. For the second voyage, Jacques Cartier was given three ships and 110 men to crew them.

---

[119] Reindeau, R., *A Brief History of Canada*. 2007.
[120] Chaves, K. and Walton, O., *Explorers of the American East: Mapping the World through Primary Documents*. 2018.
[121] Trudel, M., *The Beginnings of New France 1524 – 1663*. 2016.

Cartier's second voyage left on May 19th, 1535.[122] This time when he reached the Saint Lawrence River, he went upriver. Here, he met Chief Donnacona at the Iroquois settlement of Stadacona, and Donnacona was reunited with his two sons, who brought stories of their voyages and of their time in France.

Once there, Cartier anchored two of the three ships and sailed the smallest one farther upriver to Hochelaga, which would later be called Montreal. He was pleased to discover that Hochelaga was a vibrant place, and his ship was greeted by more than a thousand locals. However, the voyage could not proceed any farther on that course because there were rapids. They called them the La Chine (China) Rapids because they still thought they were very close to Asia. Cartier learned from the locals that there were rivers that led westward, where metals and spices could be found. Cartier headed back downriver to Stadacona in October of 1535.[123]

As winter set in, the rivers began to freeze, and Cartier decided they would need to settle there until spring before they could return to France. Cartier and his men made a fort settlement and prepared for winter by collecting firewood and stocking provisions. They hunted and fished and salted the meat to preserve it. By mid-winter, Cartier's men were all sick with scurvy and would surely have died if not for Domagaya, one of Donnacona's sons, sharing the knowledge of their spruce drink. Within days, the remaining 85 men were feeling well again. Oddly, the Iroquois had become sick at Hochelaga, where Cartier noted that fifty of them had died, and the French were blamed for this. As such, relations between the French and the Iroquois would fluctuate.

In the spring, once the ships were released from the ice in the spring thaw of May 1536, Cartier and his men prepared to return to

---

[122] Petrie, K., *Jacques Cartier*. 2010.
[123] Chaves, K. and Walton, O., *Explorers of the American East: Mapping the World through Primary Documents*. 2018.

France.[124] Cartier asked Donnacona to return to France with him, as he hoped the chief would be able to convince King Francis I of all the riches that were yet to be discovered in the New World. He called it the "Kingdom of the Saguenay" and thought they would find gold and other valuables farther north from where they'd already traveled. But Donnacona refused the offer, no matter how insistent Cartier was. Donnacona relented by offering the French a gift of four children to take with them. Cartier was not satisfied with this, however, and in the end, he kidnapped the chief anyway.

On July 15th, 1536, Cartier and his ships arrived back in France.[125] While the king was duly impressed with Cartier and Donnacona's stories and the promise of riches to come from another voyage, that third trip would not start until May 1541. There was a war going on in Europe at the time, which contributed to a delay in Cartier's next expedition. During that period, the goals of the voyage changed, and it was decided that the French would send hundreds of people to populate a settlement there instead. As for Donnacona, who had been promised passage back home, he died in France in 1539.[126]

Cartier was not completely in charge of this third voyage. Because it had now become a colonization trip, Jean-François de La Rocque de Roberval was named the first lieutenant general of French Canada and was given the lead of the expedition. Cartier was to be the chief navigator on the voyage. Cartier would sail before Roberval, however, as Roberval waited for supplies and artillery that would accompany the journey. On May 23rd, 1541, Cartier began his third voyage to Canada.[127] There were five ships this time, and the mission was two-fold. Firstly, Cartier wanted to find the "Kingdom of Saguenay," along with the riches thought to be there, and the voyage's second goal was to make a settlement on the Saint Lawrence River.

---

[124] Macauley, J., *Stirring Stories of Peace and War by Sea and by Land.* 1885.
[125] Emory, K. and Uchupi, E., *The Geology of the Atlantic Ocean.* 1984.
[126] "Cartier and Donnacona." Elementary School Resources. *Le Canada.* Web.
[127] McCoy, R., *On the Edge: Mapping North America's Coasts.* 2012.

Cartier and his men did settle the new colony. They anchored at Stadacona at first but decided to make their settlement farther upriver at what is now called Cap-Rouge, Quebec. They called their settlement Charlesbourg-Royal. They set about building a fortification and breaking land to grow vegetables. They also began gathering up the diamonds and gold found in their new settlement to send back to France.

With the work of settlement in order, Cartier traveled to Hochelaga, where he intended to continue his search for Saguenay. He encountered weather that slowed him down and discovered that the river rapids on the Ottawa River could not be navigated. Cartier returned to the settlement discouraged and discovered relations between the colonists and the Iroquois had degraded.

Cartier decided to ultimately leave the settlement in June 1542.[128] Roberval and his supplies had not even caught up to him yet. But Cartier loaded two ships with the diamonds and gold from the settlement and headed to France with the riches. He met Roberval on his way out to sea on the Newfoundland coast, and Roberval ordered him back to the settlement. Cartier, however, disobeyed the order and set sail for France in the night.

Unfortunately, when Jacques Cartier reached France in October, he would learn that the diamonds and gold they'd abandoned their mission for to bring to the king were not treasures at all. The diamonds were actually quartz, and the gold turned out to be merely iron pyrite (fool's gold).

De Roberval, however, tried to complete the mission at Charlesbourg-Royal, but the winter was very difficult, and many were lost to the cold and to scurvy. With sickness, cold weather, and rising tensions with the native people, he, too, would abandon the mission the next spring and return to France.

---

[128] Carpenter, R. *"Times are Altered with Us": American Indians from First Contact to the New Republic.* 2015.

Jacques Cartier's part of the Age of Discovery was finished. Although he discovered Canada and was the first to explore and map what would later become France's stronghold in North America, he did not discover a route to Asia, and he also did not create a permanent settlement in the New World. After Cartier's third voyage, France would not venture across the ocean to the New World for many years.

Chapter 15 – Francisco Vázquez de Coronado

As with many of the explorers and conquistadors of the day who were given top positions in the Age of Discovery, Francisco Vázquez de Coronado was from a noble family. He was born in 1510 in Spain.[129] His father was an administrator for the first Spanish governor of the Emirate of Granada, which had been the last stronghold of the Moors prior to Spanish and Castilian control. Because Francisco was not the first son, he was not going to inherit much and so was more interested in making his own fortune. With the explorations of the age, making one's fortune was often undertaken in the New World.

In 1535, Francisco Vázquez de Coronado sailed to New Spain (now Mexico).[130] He went with his friend Antonio de Mendoza, who was to be the first viceroy there. Vázquez de Coronado married well in New Spain, as his wife, Doña Beatriz, was the daughter of the treasurer of the colony. De Coronado was considered a trusted man

---

[129] Uhl, X.M. *Francisco Vázquez de Coronado: First European to Reach the Grand Canyon.* 2016.
[130] Flint, R. and Flint, S. *The Coronado Expedition: From the Distance of 460 Years.* 2003.

within the governing body, and by 1538, he was given the position as the governor of Nueva Galicia.

The Spaniards continued to explore from where they settled in New Spain. The rumors of cities of gold greatly interested the conquistadors, and Coronado was eager to explore beyond the Mexican province he governed. Between 1540 and 1542, Coronado led expeditions north into what would much later become the United States.[131] He was always in search of gold and other precious materials. On these expeditions, the Spaniards met many of the native peoples who inhabited the areas they explored.

When Coronado set out in search of the treasures of the New World, he took a huge expedition with him. The group included three hundred Spanish soldiers and up to one thousand natives (some were slaves), as well as entire herds of cattle, sheep, and pigs.

In July of 1540, Coronado came upon a Zuni settlement and met the people there.[132] The Zuni had previously encountered Spanish explorers when Cabeza de Vaca had led a smaller group into the area a year before. The Zuni had killed Estevanico, a Moroccan explorer who had been a part of Vaca's expedition and who is known to be the first African explorer of North America. As they explained to Coronado, Estevanico had been too forward with their women, and he'd demanded turquoise from them.

Coronado, unfortunately, arrived at the Zuni settlement at an inappropriate time for the Zuni, as they were in the middle of their traditional ceremonies of the summer. Besides the bad timing, Coronado went on to give the Zuni people his required speech from the Spanish Crown that they now must take on the Catholic religion and become subjects of Spain. They were told that if they did not comply, there would be a war and that after their defeat, they would become slaves to the Spaniards. The document the Spaniards read to

---

[131] Woodworth, S. *United States History: 1500 to 178 Essentials.* 2015.
[132] Bloom, L.B. and Walter, P.A., *New Mexico Historical Review.* 1971.

the people they conquered was called "El Requerimiento," which means "the requirement." It was written by Juan López de Palacios Rubios in 1513 for King Ferdinand II.[133] The protocol was to read the entire document, which was quite long and detailed, out loud to the native people. However, the document was read in Spanish, which, of course, the native people did not speak. It explained the basics of Christian beliefs and explained that they were urged to convert immediately to Catholicism.

Multiple sites have published an English translation of El Requerimiento, and the following is a small section from one of them:

> But, if you do not do this, and maliciously make delay in it, I certify to you that, with the help of God, we shall powerfully enter into your country, and shall make war against you in all ways and manners that we can, and shall subject you to the yoke and obedience of the Church and of their Highnesses; we shall take you and your wives and your children, and shall make slaves of them, and as such shall sell and dispose of them as their Highnesses may command; and we shall take away your goods, and shall do you all the mischief and damage that we can, as to vassals who do not obey, and refuse to receive their lord, and resist and contradict him; and we protest that the deaths and losses which shall accrue from this are your fault, and not that of their Highnesses, or ours, nor of these cavaliers who come with us. And that we have said this to you and made this Requisition, we request the notary here present to give us his testimony in writing, and we ask the rest who are present that they should be witnesses of this Requisition.[134]

The Zuni were not receptive to Coronado's recitation of this document, whether they understood it or not, and began to shoot

---

[133] Cowans, J., *Early Modern Spain: A Documentary History.* 2003.
[134] https://teachingamericanhistory.org/library/document/requerimiento/

their arrows at the Spaniards. The soldiers under Coronado were much better equipped to fight, however, and when they entered the settlement in retaliation, the Zuni fled.

The expedition made enemies of the native people, and they also didn't find any gold. Coronado split up the expedition and sent parties in different directions to search more. Coronado led one party to look for the city of Quivira, in what is now Kansas. Quivira was supposedly a city that held many treasures. Coronado learned of this rich city from a native they called El Turco (the Turk), who possibly made up the story in the hopes the Spanish would become lost in their pursuit of it through the wilderness. In reality, all the expedition found was a mere village of native people, possibly occupied by the Wichita people.

Another party sent off by Coronado went as far as the Colorado River and discovered the Grand Canyon. Coronado's expedition and its subsequent smaller parties covered much land in the New World and encountered many different native tribes. They covered what would become Colorado, Oklahoma, Kansas, Missouri, New Mexico, Arizona, and Arkansas. None of the exploratory parties found the treasures and gold they sought before returning to Mexico. Sometime around the early spring of 1542, Coronado received a serious injury when he fell from his horse.[135] It was there in New Mexico that Coronado decided the expedition should make its way home.

Vázquez de Coronado took up his governorship of Nueva Galicia again upon his return. The viceroy was unhappy with Coronado's expedition, however, and he was eventually found guilty of the ill-treatment of many of the native people under his command. His actions, which resulted in a huge loss of natives due to their confrontations and his demands for food and supplies from people who had little, were found to be unacceptable by the Spanish authorities. Coronado managed to escape any real punishment

---

[135] Athearn, F.J., *Land of Contrast: A History of Southeast Colorado.* 1985.

because the officials in charge were his friends. But by 1544, Coronado was sent to Mexico City and given a much lower position in the municipal government there.[136]

Vázquez de Coronado remained in Mexico City for the next ten years. He died there on September 22nd, 1554, from an infectious disease.[137]

[136] Flint, R., *Great Cruelties Have Been Reported: The 1544 Investigation of the Coronado Expedition.* 2013.
[137] Favor, L.J., *Francisco Vazquez de Coronado: Famous Journeys to the American Southwest and Colonial New Mexico. 2003.*

Chapter 16 – Francis Drake

Francis Drake was born in West Devon, England, around the year 1540.[138] At the age of eighteen, he enlisted in the Hawkins Family Fleet, whose primary work consisted of pirating foreign ships off the coast of France. He learned the craft well from the Plymouth-centered Hawkins family, eventually moving on to the African coast and taking command of his own ship in 1568.[139] Thereafter, much of Drake's income was derived from the collection and sale of kidnapped Africans to Spanish colonists in the Caribbean.

Drake was unhappy with the fact that the Spanish Empire had so much influence over his income, as its monarchs were insistent on regulating the trade of their New World colonies and seizing any contraband. Tensions between English and Spanish explorers were already very high, given the constant political strain of their respective countries, and Drake was not alone in becoming involved in violent clashes with them. Drake himself fought with a Spanish ship off the coast of Mexico. It was at San Juan de Ulúa that Drake and his crew, who were caught illegally trading there, were attacked by a Spanish

---

[138] "Sir Francis Drake." *Encyclopedia Britannica.* Web.
[139] Ibid.

ship. Managing to escape with his life, Drake returned to England in a small ship, intent on revenge against the Spanish king, Philip II.

Drake's remarkable encounter paved the way for an audience with Queen Elizabeth I, who was interested in supporting further exploits in trading throughout the New World. In 1572, he was given a privateering commission from the queen that gave him the right to pirate within Spanish lands, so long as the bulk of the proceeds were brought to the English monarch.[140] Eager to make use of the commission, Drake set sail for America in command of two ships, the *Pascha* and the *Swan.*

The primary target for Drake was the town of Nombre de Dios in modern-day Panama since it was a vital Spanish settlement full of valuable goods. Drake's crews attacked as planned, coming away with a great deal of silver, although Drake was wounded and had failed to conquer the town itself. Pressing onward and crossing the tiny expanse of Panama, it was this legalized pirate who was perhaps the first Englishman to see the Pacific Ocean.

Francis Drake returned home to England with riches enough for the queen and himself, becoming famous and wealthy all at once— however, Queen Elizabeth I had agreed upon a truce with King Philip II of Spain. The result of the treaty, at least for Drake, was that the queen could no longer openly accept the treasures he had pirated from Spanish ships. Understanding that the time for piracy was over, at least temporarily, Drake relocated to Ireland until 1577, which was when he left Britain once more to lead an expedition around South America to explore the Pacific Ocean.[141]

The Strait of Magellan was chosen as their point of entry, cutting through the southernmost tip of South America, just south of modern-day Argentina and through the bottom of Chile. This expedition, backed by Elizabeth I for the purposes of map-making and

---

[140] Ibid.
[141] Ibid.

reconnaissance, was nevertheless used by Drake as another pirating mission. There is also a theory among some modern historians that Drake's secret mission during this voyage was to discover the western side of the much-debated Northwest Passage. Beginning on the eastern side of North America in the Saint Lawrence Seaway, this mythical passage would have allowed ships to cross the New World along a watery path that stretched across Canada.

Though Drake once again had the queen's permission to destroy enemy Spanish ships and plunder the new lands, he was not specifically given leave to commit piracy. In December of 1577, he set sail with five ships and a crew of two hundred men, reaching Brazil by the spring and the Strait of Magellan on August 21st, 1578.[142] It took them sixteen days to sail to the western side and behold the Pacific Ocean. A storm hit soon afterward, and the ships were separated while struggling against high winds. After searching in vain for Drake, the commander's second-in-command, John Wynter, assumed the *Pelican*, which was later renamed the *Golden Hind*, had sunk, at which point the secondary ship turned around and headed back to England.

Alone, with all other ships having sunk or returned home, Drake and the crew of the *Golden Hind* made their way up the Pacific coast of South America. His was the first English ship in those waters, and as such, it was the only opposition to the many Spanish ships and towns he encountered there. Unprepared for unprecedented attacks in what had been Spanish-friendly waters, the Spanish ships met by Drake were quickly overpowered. At the town of Valparaíso, Drake and his crew attacked and plundered the passing ships of several Spanish merchants, coming away with bars of gold and silver, precious stones, pearls, and Spanish coins.

Laden with treasure, Drake traveled as far north as Vancouver in search of the western opening of the Northwest Passage before

---

[142] "Sir Francis Drake." *Encyclopedia Britannica.* Web.

overpowering cold weather forced him to turn back. Unable to find a waterway inland to the east, the *Golden Hind* moved south again, this time in search of potential lands that could be useful for England. Near the modern city of San Francisco, he landed and found it free of Spaniards. Naming the region New Albion, Drake claimed it in the name of Queen Elizabeth I before climbing back aboard his ship and navigating back through the Strait of Magellan. For the next year, the *Golden Hind* moved eastward, bypassing Europe to explore the waters of Asia and collect valuable goods wherever possible.

Drake returned to England via Plymouth Harbor on September 26th, 1580, his ship so full of treasures and spices that his wealth was solidified for the rest of his life. Even more treasure went to lining the coffers of Queen Elizabeth I, though. The queen was so impressed with Drake's exploits that she personally climbed aboard the *Golden Hind* and bestowed Francis Drake with a knighthood; he was known afterward as Sir Francis Drake.

Chapter 17 – Walter Raleigh and the Two Failed Colonies

Walter Raleigh was born in East Devon, England, sometime between 1552 and 1554.[143] As a young man, he was known to have participated in the civil wars in France, as well as fighting against the rebellion in Ireland in 1579. He was rewarded by the English Crown for this and was given some 42,000 acres of Irish land that had been seized by the English. Raleigh became a member of parliament in 1584, and he received the favor of Queen Elizbeth I.[144] She even knighted him in 1585 and proclaimed him the governor of Virginia.[145] Having become enamored completely by the idea of an English colony in the Americas, Raleigh sold his Irish lands and set about raising money for exploration.

Sir Walter Raleigh was given royal permission in 1584 to go on an expedition to the New World and make a settlement there.[146] His charter stated that he might rule any "remote, heathen and barbarous

---

[143] Bowling, T., *Pirates and Privateers*. 2008.
[144] Wallace, W.M., *Sir Walter Raleigh*. 2015.
[145] Moran, M., *Inventing Virginia: Sir Walter Raleigh and the Rhetoric of Colonization*. 2007.
[146] "Sir Walter Raleigh's Patent to Settle Virginia (1584)." *Encyclopedia Virginia*.

---

lands, countries and territories, not actually possessed of any Christian Prince or inhabited by Christian People."[147] The queen gave him seven years' time to settle a colony. It was hoped a strong English presence there would allow privateers to attack Spanish ships off the coast and that riches would be forthcoming from the newly settled land. Raleigh himself never sailed to North America but instead sent others to do the settling.

In 1585, Raleigh asked Sir Ralph Lane, along with Sir Richard Grenville, who was Raleigh's cousin, to sail to the Americas and try to set up a colony. They sailed from Plymouth on April 9th, 1585, with five ships: the *Tiger*, the *Roebuck*, the *Red Lion*, the *Elizabeth*, and the *Dorothy*.[148] Grenville's *Tiger* was separated from the rest of the fleet when it encountered a heavy storm near Portugal and went off course. They landed in what is now Puerto Rico and set up a camp there for several weeks before continuing on to their destination.

When Grenville's ship got to the North American coast in June of 1585, it ran aground near Wococon Island, off the coast of what is now North Carolina, and a good portion of their supplies, including valuable food provisions, was lost.[149] They went to work creating a settlement on the north side of Roanoke Island, and Grenville left Ralph Lane in charge of it as he himself sailed back to England for more supplies. The colony was not a success. Lane was not good at communicating with the native people, and there were many disagreements. There was also a shortage of necessary supplies and bad weather. By the time Sir Francis Drake arrived with a fleet, Lane and the colonists were ready to abandon their efforts and return with Drake to England. When Drake and Lane returned to England near the end of July 1586, they had brought corn, potatoes, and tobacco

---

[147] Chidester. D. and Linenthal, E. *American Sacred Spaces.* 1995
[148] Seelye, J. and Selby, S. *Shaping North America: From Exploration to the American Revolution.* 2018.
[149] Fullam, B. *The Lost Colony of Roanoke: New Perspectives.* 2017.

from the Americas.[150]

Grenville returned with supplies only weeks after the colony had been abandoned, and he decided to leave fifteen men on Roanoke Island to keep their claim on the area while he ventured off in search of Spanish treasure.

The next attempt at establishing a colony was in 1587. Raleigh put John White in charge of this journey of 115 settlers from England, who were set on creating a colony on Roanoke Island.[151] John White, the governor of this new settlement, sailed back to England to replenish supplies for the colonists on August 25th of that same year.[152] The rest of the settlers, including White's own wife and child, were left in the New World to manage and build their new home.

White returned three years later in 1590.[153] He had been delayed when Queen Elizabeth I used every ship, including White's, for the war between England and Spain. There was no sign at all of the colony by that time, except for a wooden post on which the word "Croatoan" was carved. White believed that indicated they'd moved to a nearby place by that name, but due to the bad weather, White was unable to investigate further. And so, the fates of the settlers remain unknown. Since there are no historical accounts of what occurred in that colony once White left for more supplies, it is impossible to know for sure what happened to the colonists, but there are many theories about what occurred, such as the native people wiped them out, the colonists starved, or they moved to another island where they commingled with the native people there.

Sir Walter Raleigh's efforts to create a permanent British colony in Virginia did not succeed, and there would not be one until 1604 when

---

[150] Wagner, J. and Schmid, S.W. *Encyclopedia of Tudor England.* 2011.
[151] *Time-Life Mysteries of the Unknown: Inside the World of the Strange and Unexplained.* 2015.
[152] "John White." *Encyclopedia Britannica.*
[153] Wonning, P. *Colonial American History Stories - 1763 – 1769: Forgotten and Famous.* 2017.

Jamestown (James Port) was settled by the Virginia Company of London.

Raleigh's favor with the queen suffered when Elizabeth discovered in 1591 or 1592 that he'd secretly married one of her ladies-in-waiting, Elizabeth Throckmorton, without obtaining permission first.[154] When the maid became pregnant, the secret was out. For this transgression, both he and his new wife were imprisoned at the Tower of London. Raleigh was able to purchase their freedom.

Raleigh sailed to South America in 1594 in pursuit of the "City of Gold" he had heard of. He wrote of his search for gold and this city, and his book, *The Discovery of Guiana*, was published in 1596.[155] This inflated tale is considered to be one of the reasons the legend of El Dorado became so widespread.

Raleigh eventually regained Queen Elizabeth's favor when fighting against the Spanish Armada and captured a ship from which they obtained important Spanish plans. He served as the governor of the Channel Islands and was a member of parliament for Dorset and for Cornwall.

When Queen Elizabeth I died and King James I took the throne, Sir Walter Raleigh was again imprisoned at the Tower of London, having been accused of taking part in a plot against the king. In 1616, however, Raleigh was pardoned and was sent on another expedition in search of El Dorado. When he returned, Raleigh was sent for the third, and final, time to the Tower of London, as it became known that men on the expedition, including Raleigh himself, had broken the 1604 peace treaty with Spain and plundered a Spanish post. For this, Raleigh was beheaded on October 29th, 1618.[156]

[154] Haigh, C. *Elizabeth*. 2014.
[155] Raleigh, W. *The Discovery of the Large, Rich, and Beautiful Empire of Guiana*. 1595.
[156] Graham, I. *Great Britons, A Very Peculiar History*. 2012.

Chapter 18 – The East India Trading Company

Having failed to make any serious headway in the Americas, England's Queen Elizabeth I decided to cement her kingdom's future economic success through a connection with India. On December 31ˢᵗ, 1600, she granted a royal charter to the East India Trading Company, a group of wealthy investors who were mostly from London.[157] Many of the Company's primary investors already had family money invested in merchant ships, and they believed this new project would see even higher profits than those earlier ventures.

At a time when the Spanish Navy was busy carrying tons of gold home from the New World, England's merchants desperately needed some way to keep up with the booming economy of their rivals. Already captivated by the myriad spices and aromas of India, China, and island nations of South Asia, the East India Trading Company was determined to establish a permanent trade route between England and South Asia, as well as to set up trade factories at ideal points along that path. They would have to sail around Iberia and the southern tip

---

[157] "Learning Trading Places, Timeline." *British Library*. Web.

of Africa before crossing into the Indian Ocean, which was expected to take years.

The Company's first journey east took place in 1601 on the *Red Dragon*, which was under the command of James Lancaster.[158] Three other ships made the journey under his authority, following the *Red Dragon's* lead.

> ...the first of August we came into the height of thirtie degrees south of the line, at which time we met the south-west wind, to the great comfort of all our people. For, by this time, very many of our men were fallen sicke of the scurvy in all our ships, and unless it were in the general's ship only, the other three were so weake of men that they could hardly handle the sayles. The wind held faire till wee came within two hundred and fiftie leagues of the Cape Buena Esperanza, and then came cleane contrarie against us to the east, and so held some fiteene or sixteene days, to the great discomfort of our men.[159]

It was nearly two years before the *Red Dragon* reached Aceh, Sumatra, where it put down its anchor alongside one of its companion ships. The other ships anchored at Bantam, located in Java. The English traders met other merchants from Arabia, Turkey, India, China, and Bengal there, each with their own store of goods. Expecting to trade easily with the people they encountered at these cities, Lancaster and his crew instead found it quite difficult to convince the Javanese and Sumatrans to exchange their spices for wool and iron. After all, their climate was quite different, and warm cloth was not the necessity for them as it was for the English. Desperate to get his hands on the pepper he found at Aceh, Lancaster hatched a new plan: To capture and plunder a well-stocked Portuguese ship that happened to be in the vicinity.

---

[158] Markham, Sir Clements Robert (editor). *Voyages of Sir James Lancaster.* 1877.
[159] Ibid.

The plan worked, leaving Lancaster well-stocked with gold, silver, and Indian textiles that he could use to buy the pepper he wanted. Moving on to Bantam, he found pepper at a lower price, for which he traded the fabrics he'd obtained from the Portuguese ship. Filling each of the four ships to its limit with pepper, spices, drugs, silk, carpets, porcelain, precious stones, perfume, and gourmet food items, Lancaster called the journey a success and turned around to bring the goods to London. In financial terms, the first expedition of the East India Trading Company had been a complete triumph. In human terms, however, the crew members suffered terribly during the long, isolated voyage, and many of them died along the way.

In his journal, Lancaster himself noted the extreme weakness of his and the other crews, though he records how his own crew had the benefit of the bottles of lemon juice he had brought for them to prevent scurvy. To these, Lancaster allotted three spoonsful of lemon juice each morning. His own crew, therefore, was in better health than the rest when they landed at Sumatra and Java and had to handle the unpacking of all four ships. Even the merchants, Lancaster notes, were forced to help with the sails and other regular tasks on board when the sickness was at its worst. Once the crews were together on land, Lancaster had the lemon juice administered to the ailing sailors and crews who did not serve on the *Red Dragon*, thereby treating the rampant scurvy to some degree. Still, at least a quarter of the ships' crews died.[160]

Over the following half-century, the East India Trading Company embarked upon hundreds of voyages to the East, obtaining lands in India and building trade centers in the cities of Surat, Madras, Bombay, and Calcutta. The first decades in India were fraught with challenges, the utmost one being the presence of an already-established Dutch East India Company there. Tensions grew so high

---

[160] Griffin, J.P. "James Lancaster's Prevention of Scurvy." *Journal of the Royal Society of Medicine.* 2013 Apr; 106(4): 118.

between the English and Dutch traders—as well as between other European merchants—that they collapsed into all-out warfare. The East India Trading Company originally hired Indian guards for its factories, but in a short time, there were entire armies at its disposal.

In each region in which the Company had a presence, it had a Presidency Army. These included the Presidency Armies of Bengal, Bombay, and Madras. It was due to these armies that Dutch traders were eventually driven from India altogether. They also supported the Company as the de facto ruler of most of the Indian region, leading to a historic period there known as Company Rule. The immense success of the East India Trading Company, which completely monopolized the movement of Indian goods into Europe, eventually led to the formal annexation of India by the British in 1858.[161]

[161] Stein, Burton. *A History of India.* 2010.

Chapter 19 – The Jamestown Colony

On May 14th, 1607, there would finally be a permanent settlement by the British in Virginia.[162] After Christopher Columbus began his expeditions to the New World, Spain was clearly in the lead for exploring North America. Britain was eager to establish something permanent in Virginia to put a claim to this new land. At that time, Virginia was the term used to mean the North American east coast that lay north of Florida.

Unlike Sir Walter Raleigh's attempts at establishing colonies at Roanoke, the Jamestown venture was done by a private company. King James I gave a charter to a group of people who put together the Virginia Company of London. This company had many investors, and the group planned to find gold and silver, which would make them and their investors rich, while also fulfilling their charter to the king, which was to colonize and settle the area.

---

[162] Stobaugh, J.P., *American History: Observations & Assessments from Early Settlement to Today, High School Level.* 2012.

In December 1606, the Virginia Company of London set sail with three ships and around 105 colonists, as well as their crew of 39.[163] The first of those ships was the *Susan Constant*. It carried 71 male colonists, including John Smith and Christopher Newport, the latter of which was the captain in charge of the three ships. This ship had previously been used as a rental ship carrying freight. The second ship was the *Godspeed* with Bartholomew Gosnold as captain. Aboard the *Godspeed* were 52 people. The third and smallest ship of the expedition was the *Discovery*. This ship had John Ratcliffe as its captain and carried 21 people.

The voyage from England took four months, and the ships reached the Chesapeake Bay on April 26th, 1607.[164] Once there, the three ship captains got together and opened a box that held the names of the men who were to make up the new colony's council. John Smith was supposed to be on the council, but because there were accusations against him for trying to organize a mutiny before the ships had even gotten to their destination, the council did not actually accept him for several weeks. Edward Wingfield was elected as the president of the group.

The new colonists spent some time exploring the area in order to find a place most appropriate for building the settlement. The ships were anchored in the James River, and they chose a spot where there was deep water near the shore so that ships could come in closer when they arrived, which would make loading and unloading much easier. The spot seemed to provide a natural terrain that would make it easy to defend if needed, as it was only connected to the mainland by a small piece of land. It was May 4th, 1607, that the new colony's location was decided, and the group named their new home Jamestown (or James Towne or James Fort) after King James I.[165]

---

[163] Craven, W.F. *The Virginia Company of London.* 1993
[164] Doherty, C. and Doherty, K., *Virginia.* 2005.
[165] Butman, J. and Targett, S., *New World: The Making of American by England's Merchant Adventurers.* 2018

As the business of unloading the cargo and setting about getting Jamestown established was underway, Christopher Newport decided he should take an expedition with him to see more of the rivers nearby, as there was still the overarching goal of finding a way to the Pacific Ocean. While they were away, the settlement was attacked by local natives in the area. The colonists used the cannons from the ships to fire at their attackers and successfully drove them off.

On June 22nd, 1607, Newport decided it was time to leave the settlers to their business and set sail back to England with the *Susan Constant* and the *Godspeed.*[166] He left the smallest ship, the *Discovery*, behind so colonists could use it. His report back in England was that Jamestown was in fine shape and on track to be a successful British colony.

There was a problem, though. The Jamestown colony was on land belonging to the Powhatan Confederacy and the Paspahegh tribe. However, excepting the initial attack on the newcomers, the colonists were actually generally accepted by the native people there. They were fortunate in that the tribes often supplied them with food, which the colonists often traded them for tools. Relations between the colonists and the original inhabitants fluctuated, but by 1609, the two were not on good terms.

The colonists did not have the farming skills they needed to provide for themselves, especially through the wintertime. They had not done enough work breaking and cultivating the land to grow enough food, nor had they gathered enough food to store over the winter to keep from starving. They had also failed to dig themselves a well for clean water and continued to use the water from the river, which contributed to the sickness that claimed many. John Smith and two other council members ousted Edward Wingfield from his

---

[166] Childs, D., *Invading America: The English Assault on the New World 1497 – 1630.* 2012.

position as president in hopes of making better decisions for the colony. John Ratcliffe was instead made president.

Newport arrived back at Jamestown in January of 1608, and he brought supplies and some new colonists. This expedition also brought two men who were knowledgeable in the refining of gold, as well as two men who were goldsmiths. Many of the colonists went about searching for gold, and so, for another year, the amount of farming that was needed to provide for a colony was not seen to. John Smith argued that the colony needed to focus more on work that was essential to sustain the colony. John Ratcliffe, as president, had his focus on the building of a capitol building, which many of the colonists saw as too elaborate and unnecessary. By September, John Smith took charge of the colony and immediately made a law for the people at Jamestown. "He that will not worke shall not eate (except by sicknesse he be disabled)."[167] Over the next winter, no one died of starvation.

The charter from King James I for the Virginia Company of London was changed on May 23rd, 1609, and the Virginia Company decided the colony would now be ruled by a new governor named Sir Thomas Gates. He promptly sailed from England in June of 1609 and took with him nine ships filled with supplies and new colonists. Gates' ships, the *Deliverance* and the *Patience*, were shipwrecked in a hurricane, and he and the crews were stranded on the Islands of Bermuda. The other ships reached Virginia in August. Smith was directed to step down, as the new charter had put a different governor in his place, even if the man had not yet arrived. Smith refused to leave until his term was finished, and he sailed back to England in September. George Percy took the position of governor.

It was after Smith's departure that the Powhatan Confederacy stopped their efforts to keep the colonists from starving. They instead attacked them when they attempted to trade or hunt. Because the

[167] Lincolnshire, A. Capt. John Smith, of Willoughby. 1884

colony had allowed themselves to be so dependent on the support of the tribes and had not put enough effort into their own food production, they now faced what became known as the "Starving Time," which took place over the winter of 1609-1610. During this time, 37 of the colonists escaped by ship, and only 60 colonists were left of the 500 that had been there in the fall of 1609.

On May 24th, 1610, Gates showed up with the *Deliverance* and the *Patience* after the shipwrecked crews had rebuilt the vessels and set off to Jamestown to complete their mission. Gates decided that the colony was in such bad condition that they should abandon the effort altogether. The remaining settlers were loaded onto ships, and they set sail for England on June 7th, 1610.

As they headed out, Gates and his fleet unexpectedly met a new fleet sailing into the Chesapeake Bay. This fleet held another 150 new colonists and plenty of supplies, and once again, there was a new charter that named Thomas West as the governor. West ordered Gates to return to Jamestown, and the abandonment of the permanent British colony there was averted.

Chapter 20 – The Pilgrims of the Mayflower

The Pilgrims of the Mayflower played an important role in the colonization of the New World. They did not sail to America in an effort to explore and discover so much as they were fleeing what they thought was religious persecution in Europe. They were members of a sect within the Church of England known as Puritans. Some Puritans believed they should split from the English Church, while many believed the Church simply needed reforms made to it.

As such, some of the Puritans began holding their own religious services outside the Church and acted out of the norm by having discussions about the interpretation of the Bible and allowing their parishioners to take part in church services. The Church began to fight such an attack on its power by introducing rules in 1604 that said anyone who rejected the Church of England's practices would be excommunicated and that all clergy must publicly accept the authority of the Church's prayer book.

The Pilgrims decided England was too dangerous for them now and decided Holland's more open attitude toward religious differences would be better for them. They tried to leave in 1607 but discovered they would not be allowed to go without a license. They secured a Dutch ship to sail them out anyway, but the captain betrayed them and reported them to the English authorities. They were imprisoned, but most were released after a month.

A second attempt was made to leave England in secret in the spring of 1608. Again, the group hired a Dutch ship to take them to Holland. The English authorities arrived whilst the ship was being loaded, and so, the captain set sail with only those already aboard. The rest, mostly the wives of those already aboard the ship, were arrested but later released, and they eventually made their way to Holland to reunite with their husbands.

The group lived in Holland for more than ten years. They enjoyed some religious freedom early on, but once King James I of England gained an agreement from the Dutch, saying that he would rule any English congregations in Holland, that freedom was taken away once again. The group found they were again being targeted by authorities. The only work available to them was labor-intensive textile work, and their printing equipment was destroyed to prevent them from printing their propaganda for church reforms.

The only option for true religious freedom seemed to be the New World. They debated whether Guiana or Virginia would be best and determined that Virginia was the most suitable as it was less hot and less likely to be taken over by the Spanish. They decided that they would live within the colony of Virginia but would keep themselves as a separate group.

So, the Pilgrims struck a deal with the Virginia Company. They offered to build a colony in Virginia at the mouth of the Hudson River and send supplies back to England in exchange for their voyage to the New World. They hired two ships for this venture, the *Mayflower* and the *Speedwell*. They left Holland to travel to Southampton, England, which was where they would sail from.

There was a total of 102 passengers aboard the *Mayflower*, and this number was comprised of fifty men, nineteen women, fourteen teenagers, and nineteen children.[168]

The *Mayflower* intended to accompany the *Speedwell*, which carried Pilgrims from the Netherlands, but the smaller Dutch ship had trouble on the open sea. After two quick returns to shore, the *Speedwell* was abandoned, and many of the Dutch Pilgrims climbed on board the *Mayflower*, bringing supplies from the unseaworthy boat with them for the journey. With these adjustments made, the larger ship finally departed from Southampton, England, one day later than planned, on August 16th, 1620.[169] It is difficult to pinpoint exactly how many passengers this added to the Mayflower's count. Their ultimate destination was Virginia, but storms made it impossible to reach that location. Instead, the ship landed at Cape Cod on the North American East Coast on November 21st of that same year.[170]

When the Pilgrims landed, they took it upon themselves to create a formal agreement that would govern their behavior in the new land. This agreement was the Mayflower Compact, which was signed by 41 men who had taken the journey.[171] Female settlers were not asked to sign but were expected to comply with the document, which stated the settlers would vote on their shared issues, create a constitutional law, and enact a ruling body that would legislate as the majority ruled. Everyone was required to agree before the party so much as disembarked from the ship and touched land.

The brief contract was thus:

---

[168] Scott Deetz, Patricia; and James F. Deetz. "Passengers on the Mayflower: Ages & Occupations, Origins & Connections." *The Plymouth Colony Archive Project.* 2000.
[169] Gavin, Christopher. "Plans for the 400th anniversary of the Mayflower have been announced. Here's what's happening." 18 March 2009.
[170] Gavin, Christopher. "Plans for the 400th anniversary of the Mayflower have been announced. Here's what's happening." 18 March 2009.
[171] Ibid.

In the name of God, Amen. We whose names are underwritten, the loyal subjects of our dread sovereign lord King James, by the grace of God, of Great Britain, France, and Ireland King, Defender of the Faith, etc.

Having undertaken, for the glory of God, and advancement of the Christian faith, and honor of our king and country, a voyage to plant the first colony in the northern parts of Virginia, do by these presents solemnly and mutually in the presence of God and one of another, covenant, and combine ourselves together into a civil body politic, for our better ordering and preservation, and furtherance of the ends aforesaid; and by virtue hereof to enact, constitute, and frame such just and equal laws, ordinances, acts, constitutions, offices from time to time, as shall be thought most meet and convenient for the general good of the colony: unto which we promise all due submission and obedience. In witness whereof we have hereunder subscribed our names; Cape Cod, the 11th of November, in the year of the reign of our sovereign lord King James, of England, France and Ireland eighteenth and of Scotland fifty-fourth, Anno Domini 1620.[172]

They first landed at what would become Provincetown, Massachusetts. Some of those on board went on a few expeditions, where they met indigenous peoples with whom they did not interact well. They decided it would be better to move to another spot to settle and sailed farther to Plymouth Harbor.

Because the colonists arrived in winter and were unfamiliar with the severity of this season in the New World, they were ill-prepared to survive a full winter. They set about building some shelter in January, but there were not enough supplies to build housing for everyone, and so, many lived aboard the ship for the winter. Around half of the Pilgrims died of the cold and possibly scurvy.

---

[172] Bradford, William; and Edward Winslow. *Mourt's Relation.* 1622.

What remained of the Pilgrims moved off the ship in the spring and set about settling a colony, while the ship sailed back to England. Food was a big problem for them, and without the help of the indigenous people, they would have starved. Malnutrition was one of the biggest problems they had to face through the winter. The Wampanoags assisted the settlers by showing them how to hunt, collect edible shellfish, and grow corn and beans.

The colony at Plymouth Rock was the second permanent colony in North America.

Chapter 21 - The Dutch East India Company

The Dutch East India Company (Vereenigde Oostindische Compagnie) began in 1602.[173] The Dutch wanted to get into the spice trade for themselves when they couldn't get enough spices from the Portuguese in the late 1500s. Because of high demand, the prices increased for the Dutch, causing further issues. The Dutch were in a war with Spain, and so when the Portuguese and Spanish created a union, the Dutch became more determined to obtain their own spices rather than purchase it from either Portugal or Spain.

In the late 1500s, the Dutch sent their own ships out to trade. In 1599, Jacob van Neck and his fleet were the first Dutch traders to arrive at the Spice Islands (Moluccas).[174] Even though the Portuguese had been traveling to the Spice Islands since 1512, there was room for an expanded market, and the Dutch enterprise there would profit greatly.

The Dutch Republic backed the creation of a company called the United East Indies Company, which would later become the Dutch

---

[173] Moore, C. New Guinea: Crossing Boundaries and History. 2003.
[174] Ricklefs, M.C. *A History of Modern Indonesia Since c1200*. 2008.

East India Company. The purpose of this company was to control the profits they made in the spice trade and to create a monopoly for themselves. This company was given expansive powers that allowed them to make treaties, build forts, and even employ soldiers for their own purposes.

The Dutch East India Company built the first Dutch trading post in 1603 in West Java, Indonesia.[175] They then continued to build more posts and made their main post at Ambon (Fort Victoria) and appointed Pieter Both as governor-general of the Dutch East Indies in 1610.[176] Both had first sailed to Indonesia in 1599 with four ships, and he served as governor-general until 1614. During his term, he made trade deals with the people of Moluccas and took control of Timor on the west side of the island. Both also targeted the Spanish on the island and drove them out of Tidore.

The English had also created a company for the purpose of monopolizing the spice trade, and they became the biggest competition to the Dutch East India Company until the two joined forces from 1620 to 1623. Early in 1623, however, the Dutch governor of Ambon, Herman van Speult, came to believe that the English were working against him and that they were conspiring with mercenaries and Portuguese traders to have him killed.[177] He thought that they were going to initiate this plan as soon as the next ship from England appeared so they would have some support.

Van Speult had the suspected Englishmen arrested and tortured, and they admitted to the plot and were sentenced to death. Some were eventually pardoned, but on March 9th, 1623, ten Englishmen were beheaded.[178] One Portuguese and nine Japanese mercenaries were also executed. This incident was named the Amboyna Massacre

[175] Braginsky, V. *Classical Civilizations of South-East Asia*. 2014.
[176] Crawfurd, J. *A Descriptive Dictionary of the Indian Islands and Adjacent Countries*. 1856.
[177] Fritze, R., Robison, W., *Historical Dictionary of Stuart England*. 1996.
[178] Bown, S. *Merchant Kings: When Companies Ruled the World*. 2009.

by the English, and it was the end of the cooperative efforts of the Dutch and English in Indonesia. The Dutch took the lead there when it came to trading, and they colonized the islands of Indonesia and built plantations to harvest the spices they would export.

The Dutch East India Company continued to actively expand and build trading posts throughout the years. They established a Dutch trading post at the Cape of Good Hope in Africa from which they could sell supplies to ships that were heading to Asia. They then branched out as far as Persia, Malabar, and Bengal, and by 1669, they were the wealthiest company on the planet.[179] They owned more than 150 ships, as well as 40 warships, and had their own army.

---

[179] Hebert, B. *Small World, Big Market: Global Business.* 2014.

Chapter 22 - Navigation and Mapping

The earliest maps that were made were drawings that showed coastlines, bodies of water, and topography, which were recorded two-dimensionally. During the Age of Discovery, maps of both the Old World and the New World developed exponentially. Juan de la Cosa, the cartographer who accompanied Christopher Columbus on his first and second voyage, created the first known maps of South America and North America. In 1569, a geographer and cartographer from Belgium named Gerardus Mercator put together a world map that used straight lines.[180] These lines were projected and took a round Earth into consideration, which gave navigators a way to chart their course without the distortion a map based on a flat planet had.

The Portuguese advanced their own techniques used for navigation, beginning with Prince Henry the Navigator in 1416.[181] They incorporated celestial navigation into their methods, using the sun and the stars to help them define the quadrants and latitudes they needed to set their course. Before celestial navigation, dead reckoning

---

[180] Heinrichs, A., *Gerardus Mercator: Father of Modern Mapmaking.* 2007.
[181] Russell, P., *Prince Henry 'the Navigator': A Life.* 2001.

was more prevalent. This method used a measurement of how fast the ship was traveling along with compass readings to figure out their position. What these early methods lacked was a way to determine longitude. It was not until the 1500s that an astronomer proposed a way to calculate longitude using time as part of the formula.[182]

Shipbuilders during this era also vastly improved the design of seafaring ships. Barge type ships with one square sail became more streamlined and had hulls that were stronger and able to handle rougher waters out on the Atlantic. These ships had multiple masts and more sails, which made them easier to steer.

During the Age of Discovery, the explorers learned that there were winds that affected travel on the ocean. They found that there were patterns to these winds and that sailing routes were affected by them. Christopher Columbus discovered the trade winds, and Portuguese explorers discovered the North Atlantic Gyre, a circular ocean current that affects sailing. The knowledge gained in weather patterns and winds greatly expanded the world's understanding of how the earth worked.

Another highly impactful new technology of the era was the magnetic compass. This device had already been invented several hundred years prior to the Age of Discovery, but given the relatively short journeys sailors embarked upon during those centuries, as well as the ability of navigators to plot courses by the stars, sun, and moon, compasses were hardly in fashion. Furthermore, it was customary for ships to turn back to their point of origin if clouds obscured the sky so completely that no astronavigation could be performed. That all changed when ships' captains began sailing across entire oceans and around the whole of Africa.

This little tool was first reported in Europe as early as the 12th century by a passenger on a ship named Alexander Neckam as he

---

[182] Kish, G. *A Source Book in Geography.* 1978.

crossed the English Channel:

> The sailors, moreover, as they sail over the sea, when in cloudy whether they can no longer profit by the light of the sun, or when the world is wrapped up in the darkness of the shades of night, and they are ignorant to what point of the compass their ship's course is directed, they touch the magnet with a needle, which [the needle] is whirled round in a circle until, when its motion ceases, its point looks direct to the north.[183]

Therefore, during times of inclement weather, the compass could be relied upon to reveal the position of the North Star, which was a primary focus for medieval navigators. A variety of other instruments were used on board, including the astrolabe and the cross-staff, but these were difficult to use and rely upon due to the movement of the waves and an unsteady hand. Another common tool was the quadrant, which was used with a plumb bob to measure the degree of the North Star or the sun from previous positions in the sky. One could also determine the height of mountains or hills from a distance using this device.

Captains' journals were an incredibly important part of seafaring, as these chronicled every event that took place from the point of origin until returning home. It is largely due to these in-depth journals from explorers throughout Europe that we are able to piece together what really happened during the Age of Discovery today. The journals, as well as the personal letters of Christopher Columbus, Amerigo Vespucci, and their counterparts, are the very documents upon which historians rely to recreate all those voyages and discoveries that took place so long ago.

---

[183] T. Wright, (ed.) 'Preface,' *Alexandri Neckam De naturis rerum libri duo with the poem of the same author, De laudibus divinae sapientiae.* 1893.

Chapter 23 - Food, Agriculture, and Livestock

The average European family during the start of the Age of Discovery subsisted on a diet that was high in grains and cereals. The Italians made rice-flour pasta and barley polenta, and whenever possible, they paired these with sausage and cheese. Olive was the most commonly used fat for preserving meat and fish or for frying vegetables. For most Europeans, eggs were commonly used for frittatas and omelets, while meat was a favorite—if less common—treat.

Before regular trade routes were established between Europe and the New World, most European meals comprised of grainy rye breads, simple homemade cheeses, and, whenever possible, boiled or roasted beef, pork, mutton, lamb, veal, or fish. Wine and mead accompanied the food, and a few native stone fruits, berries, and herbs filled in the gaps. To keep food edible for as long as possible, people used basic techniques such as drying, salting, smoking, and pickling.

Wheat was used to make bread for the higher classes, while oats, barley, and rye fed the lower classes and the animals. Peas, beans, and rice were also cultivated in parts of Europe. Meat was eaten as well but generally by the wealthier people. Peasants ate little to no meat, but eggs and dairy were often a part of their diet. The many different types of livestock were kept more for their aid in working the land than they were for meat.

In London and other international port cities in Europe, the people had access to foodstuffs from all over the continent, as well as the Near East. Wine was crafted and exported by France and Italy, while Ottoman and Byzantine saffron, ginger, cinnamon, and other spices made their way west via established trading routes. People of the upper and middle classes used many of these ingredients to help preserve and add flavor to a variety of dishes. Cane sugar was imported from India, while potatoes, tomatoes, hot peppers, squash, corn, and other ingredients were still an ocean away.

It was in 1537 that Spanish conquistadors first ate potatoes, which were a staple in South America.[184] These explorers brought some of the plants onto their ships and introduced the nutritious tubers to Europe during the 1550s.[185] The exotic vegetable took a long time to catch on, however, particularly since they didn't know how to cook it.

In England in 1586, Queen Elizabeth I is rumored to have been presented with potatoes by her favored navigator, Walter Raleigh.[186] In celebration of the new, highly recommended foodstuff, she gave the potatoes to her cook and planned a feast. The cook, bewildered, promptly discarded the plump tubers and served up the leaves of the plant, which did nothing to endear the potato to anyone present. Francis Drake had better luck introducing the sweet potato to the royal court, which he presented with careful instructions.[187]

The tomato was even less eagerly accepted in Europe, perhaps due to the simple mistake aristocrats made in serving the new fruit on pewter plates. Since the tomato is a particularly acidic food, its juices

---

[184] Civitello, Linda. *Cuisine and Culture: A History of Food and People.* 2007.
[185] Ibid.
[186] Ibid.
[187] Hill, Janet McKenzie. "The Boston Cooking School Magazine of Culinary Science and Domestic Economics, Volume 14." 1910.

ate into the surface of the plates and withdrew poisonous lead from the metal. Not understanding the problem, since other meals on pewter dishes went down perfectly fine, the tomato seemed the obvious culprit. For many 16th-century gardeners, tomatoes were grown as an item of exotic beauty and botanical interest, but they were certainly not for harvesting and consuming. Its resemblance to the poisonous nightshade plant was not good for its reputation, either. The ingredient fared better in Italy, where it improved classic dishes such as lasagna, formerly made with only layered pasta and cheese.

Throughout the Age of Discovery, exploratory expeditions continued to introduce new foods to the Old World. For instance, squash, tomatoes, peppers, and peanuts all came from the New World. Fruits, including pineapples, papayas, and bananas, were unknown to Europeans prior to making contact with the Americas. Not only did these new foods nourish the crews, who, after long voyages, were suffering from malnourishment, scurvy, or starvation, but they also came to feed the Europeans as well. Some were able to be grown in Europe, and the ones that could not became commodities in trade.

The attitude toward some of the new foods was not always accepting, however. Many of the foods brought to Europe were looked down upon and thought of as unappealing. This had more of an effect on the settlers in the colonies, who had to rely on local foods more than their countrymen back in Europe. Some things, such as cacao (chocolate), would gain incredible popularity and became high-priced trade goods.

After becoming fully established, and after creating modern industrial agriculture, potato crops began to quickly feed multiplying populations in Europe and allowed well-fed nations to rise to power in the 18th century.[188] Another food that became an agricultural success

---

[188] Mann, C. *How the Potato Changed the World*, Smithsonian Magazine, November 2011

once it was brought back to Europe was corn (maize), which was grown by the Mayans and other indigenous peoples. Christopher Columbus and other explorers took it back to Europe, and like potatoes, it eventually became an agricultural crop that could feed both people and livestock.

The explorers, and subsequently the colonists, brought many foods to the Americas as well. Their all-important wheat was brought and cultivated in the New World as well as other cereal crops. The Europeans also brought livestock, such as cattle, pigs, horses, donkeys, goats, dogs, and chickens. Many of these animals were originally meant for agricultural labor, as meat was considered to be expensive and therefore meant for the consumption of the higher classes. When settling the New World, however, the Europeans found vast grazing lands that could easily feed their animals, and the animals themselves soon became "crops" for the consumption of humans.

However, the land that supported these animals couldn't always support both the native and new animals. So, the colonists began to take more and more land to support their farming and animal production. Animals like pigs that the Europeans brought to the Americas foraged in the new land and took what the native species like deer ate. This led to the death of many native animals, which, in turn, affected the indigenous peoples who relied on those native animals for their own food. As such, the balance of the land had been changed forever.

The Europeans treated the land as they did back home and liked to section it off for private use. This was very different from the communal use of land that the native peoples employed. When the colonists put up fences and plowed fields in meadows, they changed the natural movement of the animals and the way the native peoples accessed the resources of the land. Suddenly, places where they'd hunted, collected water, or grew crops had been claimed and fenced off by the colonists.

The introduction of the domesticated horse to the indigenous peoples of the New World also made a huge impact. Once they saw that the horse could be used for traveling farther than usual to hunt and gather food, it was soon embraced by the native peoples. It changed the way the indigenous peoples fought as well, as horses could be used to make their warriors far faster and more powerful.

Overall, the introduction of new crops and new animals to the New World would affect the entire ecosystem of the land, and ultimately, the local environments were vastly changed. Though increased crop yields had a hugely positive effect on the human population in Europe, the human toll in the Americas was immense. Indigenous food sources were depleted quickly, and diseases from Europe ran rampant. The changes that stemmed from the actions of the explorers and colonists made permanent marks on the new land and its original inhabitants.

Chapter 24 – Disease, Slavery, and Religion

One of the worst results of the Age of Discovery was the huge loss of life of the native peoples of the New World. The indigenous peoples had no immunity for smallpox, cholera, measles, and other diseases that were carried to them by the explorers in the Age of Discovery. Such diseases were common in Europe, and in their densely populated cities, they spread easily. Because of that, there was some immunity built up against them. The native peoples in South and North America, however, had not encountered these diseases and viruses before, so when they became ill, their bodies were harder hit.

As much as 70 to 90 percent of the indigenous population was wiped out during this period of history.[189] They did not all die from European diseases, however. The conquistadors and explorers who sought gold and metals from the New World often saw fit to enslave the native inhabitants in their efforts to harvest these treasures. Many died providing forced labor to the Europeans, as they worked to extract the resources of their own lands to be taken back to the Old World.

---

[189] Jimenez, R.C. and Graeber, R.B. *The Aztec Calendar Handbook.* 2006.

The slave trade itself flourished due to the Age of Discovery. Slaves were first captured along the African coast by the Portuguese as they explored the coastline there as early as 1441.[190] These slaves were transported back to Portugal for labor, and some would even be used as labor aboard sea expeditions to the New World.

As early as 1503, the Spaniards took slaves across the ocean, and by 1518, they were taking them directly from Africa across to America.[191] As new lands became colonized and settled, the need for labor for farming, mining, and gathering of New World commodities was essential to keep their operations and further explorations going. Rather than paid labor, the free labor of slaves who'd been kidnapped from Africa and the other places the explorers discovered made up the bulk of this labor force. The more the colonies became settled, the more labor was needed, and thus, the slave trade burgeoned. Portugal and Britain were the two largest players in the transport of slaves to new destinations. The wealth created from the New World using free labor amassed great fortunes for those who sought to gain a profit, albeit at great cost to human life.

Religion was also a big part of the Age of Discovery, only because it was so intertwined with the European rulers. Dividing religion from laws or personal choices was not done back then, and disobeying the church teachings was an afront to the monarch as well. Disagreeing or practicing unauthorized religions could result in torture, imprisonment, or death.

When expeditions of discovery were authorized by Europeans monarchs, those in charge of the missions were required to convert any people they encountered. They were, in essence, claiming the new land for God as well as their king and believed, therefore, that the inhabitants of that land should worship the same way they did.

---

[190] Rodriguez, J.P. *The Historical Encyclopedia of World Slavery*. 1997.
[191] Blake, W.O. *The History of Slavery and the Slave Trade*. 1969.

The Spanish conquistadors were particularly forceful in spreading their Roman Catholic religion to the new lands they claimed. While they extracted all the wealth they could from each new place, they forced their religion on the original inhabitants. This Catholic rule was so strong that the areas colonized by Spain are mostly Catholic to this day.

The Church of England, which is a branch of Protestant Christianity (Anglican), was in religious control of the first colonies in Virginia. Within that group, there were religious dissenters, such as the Pilgrims. As the diversity of the settlers in that part of the New World increased, however, there eventually developed a broader range of religions in what would one day become the United States. Some even found they were religiously persecuted by the Puritans, who themselves had come to the New World to escape just that. By the 17th century, there were Baptists, Congregationalists, Quakers, and Presbyterians in the English colonies, while Catholicism was predominant in the Spanish and French colonies.

The beliefs and religious practices of the native peoples who already existed in the places that were colonized were not considered acceptable by the newcomers. They were thought to be far inferior to the European religions and were completely overrun by the colonists' belief that their own religion must be spread to the natives. Due to that, many traditions and much knowledge of the native religions were lost.

As colonies grew and Europeans took more and more control of the New World, they made laws and rules in their governments that were based on their religious beliefs, making any other way of life illegal and criminal. The immense continents to the west of Europe were forever changed once colonization took hold, as were the lives of everyone on both sides of the Atlantic Ocean.

Epilogue

It is insufficient to say that the Age of Discovery changed the world. The sheer vastness of the earth was entirely unprecedented by anyone living in relatively tiny Europe, which meant that the number of potential friends, enemies, and trading partners could explode after one journey abroad. Firstly, the most obvious change was the map and the known geography of the world. General knowledge began to accept that the world was larger than imagined and that it was probably not flat, meaning traveling beyond certain points did not mean certain death. The explorers ventured further and further and mapped more and more land and waterways that would become major destinations and well-traveled routes. As a result, the art of navigation grew by leaps and bounds during this time.

Most importantly, Europeans had the specific knowledge necessary to quickly exploit their new neighbors into providing them with free labor, free gold, and free land. The economies of the countries and monarchies that took over lands and trading routes were changed for the better, particularly Spain, Portugal, England, and France. They sought and found places with gold, metals, spices, and foods that became commodities and trade goods both on the world market and in their own home markets. The Spanish cane sugar plantations of Hispaniola boomed, becoming the main source of sugar for all

Europeans. The Spanish Empire, which was united by Ferdinand and Isabella, became a more tightly-knit community based on their shared belief in Catholicism and Spain's position as Christ-bearer, as Columbus came to call himself.

However, many died in the pursuit of discovery. Millions of sailors died of scurvy or starvation while far from home in foreign lands. Others were lost at sea or killed in wars over trade routes or new borders. Huge numbers of indigenous peoples also died from new diseases, warfare, and slavery, and native animals died from a lack of food, as the newcomers helped themselves to the natural resources they depended on.

Monopolies on trade and commodities took a firm hold during this time in history, as companies were formed specifically to organize and run monopolies on the trade of spices and goods from the New World. The immense fortunes made by those companies, and by the countries that fought and won trade access, helped to build European societies that flourished due to the plunder of these new lands and the people living there.

For instance, the slave trade, which kidnapped people from Africa and transported them to the New World as a means for free labor, exploded during the Age of Discovery in order to satisfy the intense need for workers by the colonists. Europeans, working under the strict beliefs and laws of their respective Christian churches, believed that human trafficking was fair game since the people they enslaved were categorized as heathens.

That said, the seeds of religious freedom began to take root in the American colonies near the end of the era, as settlers sought less restriction on their spiritual lives. The Mayflower Pilgrims are a prime example of that movement, but they were far from the only ones. Still to come were the Pennsylvania Germans, Deists, Mormons, Baptists, Methodists, and numerous forms of Protestant Christianity.

The Age of Discovery may have brought about the first real steps toward globalization, but it did not come without great cost. From a purely human perspective, it was the Europeans who clearly benefited from their discovery of a whole new world of resources. Their royal coffers were filled with gold, and their merchants' ships were piled high with sugar and tobacco, while groups of people like the Taíno, unfortunately, have been virtually wiped from the face of the earth.

Here's another book by Captivating History that you might be interested in

CPSIA information can be obtained
at www.ICGtesting.com
Printed in the USA
LVHW081309130521
687348LV00002B/33